THE WASHINGTON PAPERS

... intended to meet the need for an authoritative, yet prompt, public appraisal of the major developments in world affairs.

President, CSIS: David M. Abshire

Series Editor: Walter Laqueur

Director of Publications: Nancy B. Eddy

Managing Editor: Donna R. Spitler

MANUSCRIPT SUBMISSION

The Washington Papers and Praeger Publishers welcome inquiries concerning manuscript submissions. Please include with your inquiry a curriculum vitae, synopsis, table of contents, and estimated manuscript length. Manuscripts must be between 120–200 double-spaced typed pages. All submissions will be peer reviewed. Submissions to *The Washington Papers* should be sent to *The Washington Papers*; The Center for Strategic and International Studies; 1800 K Street NW; Suite 400; Washington, DC 20006. Book proposals should be sent to Praeger Publishers; One Madison Avenue; New York NY 10010.

I DON'T BRUISE EASILY

THE AUTOBIOGRAPHY OF
BRIAN CLOSE

written in association with Don Mosey

MACDONALD AND JANE'S · LONDON

Printed in Great Britain by
Hazell Watson and Viney Limited
Aylesbury, Bucks

CONTENTS

The Washington Papers/136

The Dreadful Fury

Advanced Military Technology and the Atlantic Alliance

Michael Moodie

Foreword by Senator Sam Nunn

Published with The Center for
Strategic and International Studies
Washington, D.C.

New York
Westport, Connecticut
London

Library of Congress Cataloging-in-Publication Data

Moodie, Michael, 1948–
    The dreadful fury : advanced military technology and the Atlantic
Alliance / Michael Moodie ; foreword by Senator Sam Nunn.
        p.   cm. – (The Washington papers, ISSN 0278-937X ; 136)
    "Published with the Center for Strategic and International Studies,
Washington, D.C."
    Includes index.
    ISBN 0-275-93236-2 (alk. paper). – ISBN 0-275-93237-0 (pbk. :
alk. paper)
    1. North Atlantic Treaty Organization – Armed Forces.   2. Europe –
Military policy.   3. Technology and state – Europe.   4. Military art
and science – Europe – History – 20th century.   5. Munitions – Europe.
I. Center for Strategic and International Studies (Washington,
D.C.).   II. Title.   III. Series.
UA646.3.M63 1989
355′.031′091821 – dc19   88-38059

The *Washington Papers* are written under the auspices of The Center
for Strategic and International Studies (CSIS) and published
with CSIS by Praeger Publishers. The views expressed in these papers
are those of the authors and not necessarily those of the Center.

Library of Congress Catalog Card Number: 88-38059
ISBN: 0-275-93236-2 (cloth)
        0-275-93237-0 (paper)

First published in 1989

Praeger Publishers, One Madison Avenue, New York, NY 10010
A division of Greenwood Press, Inc.

Printed in the United States of America

The paper used in this book complies with the Permanent
Paper Standard issued by the National Information Standards
Organization (Z39.48-1984).

10   9   8   7   6   5   4   3   2   1

Contents

Foreword

For many years, I have argued that the NATO Alliance has poorly translated the West's technological innovations in the laboratory into effective weapons systems on the battlefield. And NATO has not thought creatively enough about ways to exploit its enormous technological prowess to foster truly revolutionary changes in warfare. NATO has also been unable to resolve satisfactorily the tension caused by the competing imperatives to share technology among alliance members and to protect technology from leaking to NATO's adversaries.

The sources of NATO's failure to forge an effective coalition for technology strategy are not difficult to identify. Among the most serious are

- competition among economies driven by visions of strong growth led by robust high-technology sectors;
- a badly fragmented alliance defense industrial infrastructure; and
- a poor appreciation for the tapestry of strategy that weaves technology together with other critical determinants of effective performance in war.

Because NATO's adversaries are reducing the qualitative advantage on which the alliance has traditionally relied to offset its numerical inferiority, there is an urgency to correcting NATO's shortcomings in its exploitation of technology. More and more, we hear that new systems entering the Soviet inventory are comparable to and, in some cases, better than equipment fielded by NATO forces. Admittedly, new Soviet systems are not as good as those on NATO's drawing boards. That should give little comfort, however, because the war will not be fought in the laboratories, and NATO nations have been slow to transform drawings into systems.

NATO policymakers should also be driven to develop a more cohesive approach to technology decisions because they will have to be made in a future environment that is even more complex and fast-moving. Without an agreed-upon framework, those decisions are not going to be easier, and the possibilities both for mistakes that cost millions (if not billions) of dollars and for political disputes that chip away at alliance cohesion will multiply. If technology discussions can be removed from the agenda of disputes through the development of a coordinated approach, NATO will be better able to deal with other disagreements that will inevitably arise.

Michael Moodie's essay is an important contribution to the better understanding of these issues. Its greatest strength is the way in which it assimilates many issues usually treated separately and relates them through the concepts of "alliance technology management" and a "technology management strategy." Its prescriptive sections are timely, practical, and deserving of widespread consideration throughout the alliance.

Technology will obviously not solve all of NATO's problems. In the major wars of this century, technology alone has never been the decisive factor determining the victor and the vanquished. But technology is too precious an asset for the Atlantic Alliance to squander. Across the spectrum of developing and applying technology, NATO must do better. The starting point is better thinking about technology's relationship to other pieces of the NATO mosaic. This book is a good place to begin.

Sam Nunn
Chairman
Committee on Armed Services
United States Senate

January 1989

Preface

During three and a half years as special assistant to the U.S. ambassador to NATO, the author had an opportunity to see first hand the way the Atlantic Alliance struggled to come to grips with the challenges posed by the current explosion of technology across the globe. The impact of that explosion was pervasive, affecting the entire list of issues on the alliance agenda either directly or indirectly. In that struggle, NATO was sometimes successful, such as in the development of the Conceptual Military Framework to guide NATO planning decisions for the next 20 years or the renewed momentum to secure greater alliance armaments cooperation fostered by efforts of individuals on both sides of the Atlantic. Sometimes, however, the struggle failed; some initiatives that held promise just faded away, while others were actively stalemated.

The seeds of this effort were sown by both that failure and that success. The failure demonstrated how much remained to be done; the success, what could be accomplished. In that sense, the message of this analysis is one of hope, not despair.

The author would like to thank the Lynde and Harry Bradley Foundation and the Sarah Scaife Foundation for sponsoring the CSIS project on a defense investment strategy for the United States and its allies, under whose auspices this book has been completed.

The author has also been helped enormously by a host of people in bringing this manuscript to completion. Deserving special thanks, however, are David Abshire, who provided in Brussels the encouragement to tackle the issue in the first place and in Washington the opportunity to see it through to conclusion; David Hobbs, whose willingness to engage in long conversations and, more important, whose friendship helped the author sort out his thinking and kept him from straying too far; Brent Fischmann, who allowed the author to make use of their joint work on arms cooperation without really taking adequate credit; Sam Taylor, Chris Stoch, and Dexter Congbalay for their work on the case studies and their willingness to read early versions; and Connie O'Reilly for her tireless and good humored battles with a seemingly never quite finished manuscript. It goes without saying that final responsibility for the content is mine alone.

About the Author

Michael Moodie, senior fellow at the Center for Strategic and International Studies (CSIS), returned to CSIS in 1987 after nearly four years as special assistant to the ambassador at the U.S. mission to NATO. Prior to serving with USNATO, Mr. Moodie was chief program officer at CSIS, where he was also associate editor of the *Washington Quarterly*. A specialist in security affairs, he has served as a consultant to the President's Foreign Intelligence Advisory Board and has written on a wide range of issues including NATO, arms transfers, and Third World defense industries.

He is the author of *Sovereignty, Security, and Arms* and coauthor of *Geopolitics and Maritime Power*, both Washington Papers. He has also coauthored *NATO: The Next 30 Years* in the CSIS Significant Issues Series, and *The President, Congress, and U.S. Global Leadership*, a Washington Quarterly White Paper. In addition, his articles have appeared in such publications as *NATO Review, History and Modern Strategy,* and *Seapower*. He holds a master's degree from the Fletcher School of Law and Diplomacy at Tufts University.

Summary

In an era of unprecedented technological change, how can NATO best exploit advanced technology to bolster its conventional forces on the battlefield of the future? That is the central question of this book. It is a unique analysis integrating the political, military, economic, and technological factors shaping the tough choices confronting Atlantic Alliance policymakers as they attempt to maximize the impact of one of NATO's greatest assets. After a brief review of the nature of technological change in the modern age, the book examines the shifting industrial landscape within which that change occurs. It then addresses the key problems alliance policymakers must confront in such critical areas as technology transfer, allied cooperation in development and procurement of modern arms, and the impact of new technology on the conduct of war. Drawing on the author's experience at NATO Headquarters, the book's focus on alliance rather than national perspectives of military technology provides an unusual approach to one of the most difficult challenges facing NATO today. In the book's final chapter, a package of policy recommendations is offered to help chart a steady NATO course through the turbulent 1990s.

The Dreadful Fury

Introduction

The Atlantic Alliance faces a resources crunch. Every NATO ally confronts severe political and economic pressures to limit defense spending. Faced with tight financial constraints, NATO allies, including the United States, are likely to undertake a fundamental review of their national security programs and commitments. As a result, the prospect looms of a widening gap between NATO's requirements for deterrence and defense and the resources allies are willing to commit to secure them. If NATO is to get the most out of its limited defense resources, the alliance urgently needs a new approach that coordinates and harmonizes national resource choices.

One resource that will make a critical contribution to NATO's future success is advanced technology. That NATO offsets its quantitative disadvantage with qualitative advances gained through better technology has become a cliché. As with most clichés, however, the statement is true, but its superficial reality does not capture the deeper and more profound phenomena at work. How NATO nations exploit their enormous technological prowess in the future will be a critical issue for alliance policymakers. It is not one, however, that will be easy to manage. NATO urgently needs a technology management strategy.

A primary reason for the difficulties technology creates in relations among NATO members is that technology's impact extends well beyond the military arena to other areas in which the NATO security allies are also intense economic competitors. Technology has been identified as the engine powering a transformation of the world economy that is as significant as the industrial revolution of the last century. Technology is viewed as so important to the future prosperity of the industrial democracies that it has created high stakes for which all of the NATO allies are playing. As a result, technology itself—how it is developed, exploited, shared, and protected—has become a source of continual tension and frequent grievance among allies.

Another problem arises because the industrial democracies are security partners. If the NATO allies are to meet the challenge of bringing high technology to the battlefield in a timely and cost effective manner, they can do so only as a coalition. The fact that future battlefields will be allied battlefields demands the integration of technology into forces that will fight together in ways that complement the performance of all. This is not easy in an alliance of 16 sovereign members, whose individual competence differs when it comes to advanced technology, whose historical military traditions suggest individual ways in which technology should be applied, and whose approaches to technology's commercial exploitation often vary markedly.

Yet just such an integration is more critical today than ever before, not only because of the tough choices imposed by constrained resources. Areas of defense weakened by inadequate technological capabilities—or other shortcomings for that matter—are ripe for exploitation, and NATO's potential adversaries in the Warsaw Pact are increasingly capable of such exploitation. The Pact not only enjoys superior numbers in most major weapons categories, but also has been gradually closing the technology gap that existed between itself and NATO since the creation of the two alliances.

On a head-to-head basis, NATO technology remains superior, but in some areas of technology in which NATO nations enjoyed a lead of a decade or more, that advantage has been shortened to two to three years. When does that technological edge become so small that it can no longer compensate for NATO's inferiority in numbers? As Senator Sam Nunn has pointed out, it is necessary for the NATO allies to do better in coordinating and integrating their advanced technology research and development efforts if the alliance is to witness the "revolution" in conventional capability necessary to undermine the Warsaw Pact's growing capability – both quantitative and qualitative.

To make the most of what technology has to offer, NATO policymakers must achieve two fundamental objectives. First, although they must recognize that technology is not a military panacea, they must nevertheless maximize technology's contribution to military performance. This will be accomplished by rapidly identifying the impact that advanced technologies can have on the battlefield, introducing those technologies quickly and efficiently into the alliance force structure, and integrating new technologies with appropriate changes in organization, operations, and tactics.

Second, allies must minimize technology as a source of political friction. As long as differences exist among allies about how technology is to be developed, used, and only then shared and applied to their respective military forces, NATO's ability to achieve its first objective will be consistently undermined.

To achieve these two objectives, NATO leaders must answer four challenging questions:

• How can NATO cope with today's broad and rapid process of technological change, a process that has altered beyond recognition during the 40 years since NATO's creation?

• How can NATO's military structures adapt organizationally, operationally, and tactically to get the best out of what advanced technology has to offer for the battlefield of the future?

• How does NATO reconcile the equally valid policy goals of sharing technology with allies while protecting itself from adversaries?

• How does NATO organize its defense industrial effort to be responsive to the complex process of technological change?

These questions are examined in more depth in the following four chapters. After the first chapter reviews the current advanced technological environment, each of the next three addresses the more military questions of direct concern to NATO policymakers. Each of these three chapters is preceded by a case study that highlights some of the major problems and issues. The final chapter suggests that if NATO is to find an answer to these tough questions, it will require some fundamental changes in the alliance's "business as usual."

1

The Changing Technological Environment

"Blessed be those happy ages that were stranger to the dreadful fury of those devilish instruments of artillery, whose inventor, I am satisfied, is now in hell receiving the reward of his invention"—Cervantes, *Don Quioxte*

One of the singular characteristics of the late twentieth century is its complex and rapidly changing technological environment. At perhaps no time in man's history has technology changed so rapidly across such a wide variety of areas. If the Atlantic Alliance is to exploit the potential inherent in its prodigious technological capabilities fully, it must be responsive to that environment. For an alliance of 16 nations that will not be an easy task.

The current technological environment exhibits a variety of tensions such as competition versus cooperation among allies, civilian versus military applications, and research versus development. One of the greatest challenges to NATO in developing and implementing an effective technology management strategy will be to reconcile those tensions. An appreciation of the contours of that technological environment provides a rough map for charting the way ahead.

Two features of the current environment that particularly need to be addressed are the process of technological change and the technological industrial scene. Together these features shape the terrain of the complex environment of change in which alliance policymakers must act.

The Process of Technological Change

The process by which scientific knowledge is translated into usable civilian and military items, and vice versa, has become increasingly complicated. The complexity of the contemporary technology development process derives from the interaction of several characteristics.

The Subsystem Focus

Rather than finished systems—whether tanks or televisions—many of today's technological advances in both the civilian and the military sectors occur at the component or subcomponent level. The same semiconductors and computer software can have multiple uses. New materials can be incorporated into a variety of products.

The pervasive impact of subcomponent development in the military sphere is exemplified by the very high speed integrated circuit (VHSIC). It has been claimed that VHSIC technology, which is now being inserted into new electronic systems, will provide an order of magnitude increase in computation ability, use only 20 percent of the power now required, be one-fourth the size and weight of existing circuits, cost one-tenth the price, and be at least 10 times faster than current circuits.[1]

The implications of such enhanced capability are obvious. Incorporation of VHSIC in the firing and tracking systems of the TOW-2 antitank weapon, for example, will allow the weapon to fire, track, and guide two missiles while tracking two targets.[2] Other applications include incorporation in the U.S. Air Force's AN/ALQ-131 jamming pod, the Patriot and Hellfire missiles, signal processors for antisubmarine warfare, and the advanced lightweight torpedo.

Given the initial success of the VHSIC program, the Pentagon hoped to develop a "superchip," one of the most complex devices ever built, packing 28 million transistors into a 1.4 square inch area. Although design problems have forced the Department of Defense (DOD) to reduce its ambitions, a new chip will still contain the unique feature of a form of on-chip redundancy that makes it self-correcting.[3]

Even VHSIC, however, is not the ultimate state of the art in this area of subcomponent design. As Westinghouse's Richard Linder has pointed out, "Large scale integration (LSI) chips advanced the capability and shrank the size of avionics in the 1970s, . . . VHSIC continued that growth in the 1980s, and wafer-scale integration will be the avionics technology of the 1990s," leading to further advances in both speed and reliability.[4]

Another longer-term subcomponent development with potentially enormous application is the superconductor. When they make their appearance, these systems could be applied to such diverse areas as ultralight propulsion of submarines, hardened infrared sensors, high-capacity transmission lines, and electromagnetic launchers, among others.

One aspect of this more decentralized technology development process that has received attention in recent months is new "nanotechnology," which promises smaller, faster computer chips that contain millions of logic elements, microrobots, and microscopic sensors.[5] Recent experiments have involved structures measured in nanometers — one billionth of a meter — the size of some large molecules. Researchers have already produced a semiconductor laser 10,000 times smaller than the smallest available today. In March 1988, at the Siemens Laboratory and Cornell, the world's fastest transistor was built, capable of switching 113 billion times per second. Its electronic gate was etched with an electron beam the width of 300 gold atoms.[6]

The range of application of this microtechnology appears limitless. The ability to shrink circuit size, for example, means smaller, denser, and smarter computers, an obvious advantage in many areas of civilian and military activity.

The implications of development of subcomponent technology run far beyond the number of military uses such technology might have. There are economic and, hence, political considerations as well. More economic enterprises can play in the game. A 1986 survey of U.S. high-technology industries, for example, indicated a major increase in the growth of capabilities outside Silicon Valley in northern California, the region traditionally synonymous with electronics advances. Areas that were giving Silicon Valley a run for its money included the Boston region, Orlando, Florida, Texas, and southern California.[7] In many cases that growth was prompted by development of customized integrated circuits, often for the military.

Smaller innovative entities can provide services globally. In turn, by encouraging innovation, greater risks might be taken because the stakes are not necessarily all or nothing, as would be true if development proceeded on the system level. Multiple applications for components can represent multiple sources of profit. Newly developed components or subcomponents should be able to be introduced relatively swiftly into existing systems, making system upgrades more feasible and potentially more cost effective than the introduction of entirely new systems.

The decentralized nature of this component focus of technological development, however, also creates a difficult environment for effectively exploiting explosive change. It produces unprecedented rates of advance leading to shorter product life cycles. Given the increasing time it takes to get a full system such as an airplane or tank into the field, this speed and short product life cycle could make a system obsolete before it enters service.

The decentralization of the technology development process is embedded in the decentralization of the industrial sector with the proliferation of smaller, highly competitive firms at technology's cutting edge. Some of these firms will win big, and others will lose. If a national system prohibits failure, as many of the industrial systems in Europe seem to do, government assistance that keeps sick companies and industries alive will foster uncompetitiveness in the world market. The impact could be to undermine the robust industrial base on which the West's security ultimately depends. How this situation might be affected by Europe's push to a single market by 1992 and the concomitant move toward larger, pan-European firms remains to be seen. There does appear to be the beginning of rationalization in Europe's high-technology industries, such as electronics, despite the potential negative effects in some countries.

Another possible problem with subcomponent-led technology development is that of integration. Given the plethora of available components, a finished system could become a conglomeration of parts that do not necessarily fit together, thereby degrading performance. The concurrent increases in processor capability, shrinking component size, and advances in composites and conducting plastics, however, enable dramatic improvements in system architecture that could overcome some of these potential difficulties.[8]

The Broad Scope of Change

The scope of current technological change is breathtaking, from microelectronics to composite materials, from robotics to life sciences and biotechnology. This development of technology across a broad spectrum is often simultaneous, interrelated, and overlapping, imposing a need to take an integrated approach to decisions about which technologies will be emphasized and how they will be exploited.

One area that is especially critical because it affects every aspect of life and, hence, every aspect of the security arena is electronics. Electronics is perhaps the single most important force multiplier available to the West, whether it is in enhancing the capabilities of individual weapons, improving critical ancillary functions such as target acquisition, or assisting in the design and production of future systems.

The potential impact of electronics is clearly recognized, of course; witness the fact that by 1996, between 30 percent and 35 percent of the U.S. procurement budget is expected to be electronics-related. As a result, the United States will spend more money on electronics than some countries will devote to their entire defense budget. The DOD now spends more on computers and software, for example, than the United Kingdom spends in total on defense.[9] In some cases, the DOD is assigning prime contracts to electronics houses, rather than to the larger defense companies such as major airframe companies that traditionally hired the electronics firms as subcontractors. In Europe, more than 50 percent of the cost of each European Fighter Aircraft (EFA) will be accounted for by airborne electronics systems.[10]

Industry recognizes the heightened importance of electronics. Given that spending for electronics will remain high, "it seems every defense-electronics player is either buying someone else or being bought – a process that spans the Atlantic." More than two dozen acquisitions have occurred in the past two years.[11]

The problems NATO policymakers must confront in applying electronics, however, are its rapidly growing cost and excessive production duplication. A vibrant electronics sector has become a sine qua non for a nation to be considered an advanced industrial power, and developing or sustaining such a capability is a high priority in most alliance countries. This includes a country like Turkey that is relatively less industrially developed than other NATO allies. Turkey is intent, however, on rapidly improving its electronics industry as a way of pulling along other advanced industrial sectors.

Another technological area in which the speed of developments has been remarkable is the field of new materials. The materials revolution is based on clay, plastic, and sand; yet, from these mundane substances, man is creating new materials such as fine ceramics (not to be confused with high-quality bone china) and high-performance plastics that are harder, stronger, lighter, more durable, and cheaper than many metals.[12] These materials, and the advanced composites to which they contribute, promise to transform both products and production processes.

Aerospace has already felt the impact of new materials, including military aircraft. Already, 30 percent of the airframe and wings of the AV-8B Harrier vertical/short takeoff and landing (V/STOL) airplane is made of composite materials,[13] and both U.S. "Stealth" aircraft and the EFA will incorporate composite materials to a significant degree.

Other areas in which rapid technological change is proceeding are biotechnology and life sciences, transportation improvements, and information technology, including telecommunications and information processing. Indeed, some observers would contend that it is the information revolution that is the singular feature driving the entire technology revolution now being experienced. Fiber optics, for example, which transmit enormous chunks of data in pulses of light, promise to put more information into more hands than ever before.[14] Artificial intelligence including "expert system" technology will permit the mechanization of practical knowledge and human reasoning in many fields.[15]

The direct impact of some of these changes on the battlefield may not yet be apparent. How life sciences, for example, will affect demographic patterns – an important but too often neglected consideration in force planning – may not be known for decades. What is clear, however, is that, taken together, the rapid change that is occurring across this broad range of technology is already shaping a global transformation. It is in that changing global context that NATO policymakers will face some very tough choices.[16]

Merging Technologies

The third characteristic of the process of technological change is what François Heisbourg, director of the International Institute for Strategic Studies (IISS), has called "merging technologies." Heisbourg describes this trend as "the increased technical commonality between what used to be completely different functions; for example, sensing, fusing, processing, transmitting, and distributing information are all functions that tend to merge within information systems, civilian or military."[17]

Merging technologies simplify action and potentially reduce the amount of manpower needed to perform a given set of functions. It does pose some problems, however. As Heisbourg argues, "the fusion of information and communication technology in the civil and military (C^3I) fields will make it conceptually and technically difficult to deal with weapons systems and macrosystems as discrete entities."[18] At the very least, such a development will have important consequences for NATO at the level of the organization of its forces, a factor too often ignored in technology-related decisions.

New Industrial Processes

Computer integrated manufacturing (CIM) is the essence of new production techniques based on advanced technology that are revitalizing manufacturing itself. Indeed, the argument has been made that the new battle of manufacturing competitiveness and productivity is going to be fought in the fields of process and design technology. "Smart machinery," for example, has been described as "the key element in competitiveness" in the future.[19]

CIM is based on flexible, multipurpose shop that can run 24 hours a day, but which can be reprogrammed in a matter of minutes to turn out a completely different product. This flexibility is CIM's key attraction, and the improvements in production it makes possible include increased reliance on robotics, greater utility of industrial lasers, and new shaping techniques. These developments tend to reduce labor costs and foster rapid adaptation to the changing market. They also prompt shorter production runs, minimal inventories, and enhanced economies of scale.

Defense industries in alliance countries will not remain immune to the impact of new manufacturing techniques. At the very least, as in other areas of manufacturing, they could lead to increased competitiveness among defense firms. If defense industries can take full advantage of the range of benefits that CIM and similar developments have to offer in terms of efficiency and elimination of waste, those developments would have made an important contribution to the alliance's ability to move technological innovation from the laboratory drawing board into the field of combat.

The Blurring of Distinctions

As a consequence of the speed, scope, and impact of technological change, the lines traditionally drawn between technology and other endeavors, such as science, are beginning to blur, as are the lines between civilian and military technology.

Frank Press, president of the American National Academy of Sciences, has argued that "there are no boundaries any more" between science and technology.[20] He notes that for two successive years, the Nobel Prize in physics has gone to industrial scientists. Superconductivity is being pursued in both academic laboratories as well as those of commercial enterprises such as IBM or Bell Labs. The drive toward miniaturized technology and work on new materials are also blurring the traditional distinction between science and technology because both of them operate on the level of molecules, if not even smaller entities.

Interdisciplinary approaches that promise to foster fundamental changes in the university environment constitute yet another factor. These changes are prompted by new disciplines spawned by advanced technology, which, in fact, combine several traditional disciplines. According to Dr. John Baras, director of the Systems Research Center at the University of Maryland, "Systems have become so complex that it's virtually impossible for any single discipline to handle an entire problem."[21]

The line between those technologies that have only a military application and those that will remain in the civilian sphere has also blurred. Everything is becoming "dual use." The same components can be used in many cases for a tank and a tractor. Moreover, today it is most often the commercial marketplace, rather than military requirements, that spurs new technological development, and it is the military that seeks the commercially generated result.

The military can still make important contributions to technological development. The *Economist* notes, for example, that the U.S. Defense Advanced Research Projects Agency (DARPA) has been extremely active in promoting exotic high-technology development programs in computers, communications, and electronic equipment generally. It estimates that DARPA's VHSIC project alone cost $300 million in the five years prior to 1986 and that the agency would spend a reported $1 billion on supercomputer technology.[22]

The increasing merger of civilian and military technology has created the concern in some quarters, however, that in the future it will be much more difficult to control the dissemination of militarily significant technologies because of their availability in the civilian sector. Accelerating advances in computer technology, telecommunications, and information processing are both reducing the importance of geographic distance and making applied research and technological expertise more rapidly and more widely available. Such trends are likely to continue. As a result of such pressure, efforts to restrict the flow of technology or information will become increasingly difficult.

The Sum of the Trends: Accelerated Change

Economic analyst Harald B. Malmgren points out that, "Running throughout all of these historic forces of change is the compression of time, the acceleration of change."[23] He also notes "the economic behaviour patterns, which presently are embodied in institutional and political processes of decision making, are very time sensitive." There is a "congenital tendency . . . to stretch out the time taken for change," to slow things down, and actively retard the process of structural change.[24]

Like economic entities, the military also requires time to evaluate new ideas and assess their potential. Like economic entities, however, the military also faces an accelerating pace of change that is speeding product obsolescence, shortening the time required to produce new services or a new good embodying a new idea, and hastening the international dissemination of information and technology.

Clearly, an environment in which time for decisions is shortening exacerbates the pressure on the military's decision-making process. There will be an increased need for faster response and faster adaptation of defense production processes. In NATO's case, the difficulty is complicated by the fact that the process must be accommodated by 16 sovereign nations that must work together. Whether NATO's current structure is capable of such coordination within a period of increasingly compressed time for reaction is open to question.

The Industrial Environment

The second major factor shaping the current international high-technology environment is the global industrial landscape. As companies and countries confront the internationalization of high technology, the major characteristic of that landscape is its increasing competitiveness. Rightly or wrongly, high technology has come to be seen as a major drive behind economic growth. All nations fear they might be unable to compete. With firms around the world – supported by governments of the countries from which they operate – intensifying their efforts to expand their shares in the global high-technology market, that competition could become not only an economic issue, but also a political problem.

Because the NATO allies are economic competitors as well as security partners, NATO's decisions about technology will be judged – and made – partially in this competitive light. To have an accurate picture of the overall environment, however, it is important to understand the problems and prospects not only of U.S. and European high-technology industry but also of Japan, another crucial player in the game.

In recent years, the high-technology industrial sector has been characterized by growing European concern about an unbridgeable technology gap between Europe on the one hand and the United States and Japan on the other, by perceptions of a relative decline of U.S. high-technology leadership, and by images of a Japanese high-technology juggernaut unstoppable in its drive for global domination at least of the consumer goods market. Are these perceptions correct? Are the Europeans as bad as they sometimes think? Are the Japanese as good? Where does the United States stand?[25]

There is no doubt that Japan has become a considerable force in the global high-technology market. It has not been alone, however; recent years have also witnessed the emergence of other Asian "tigers" – notably South Korea, Taiwan, and Singapore, with Thailand beginning to become more active in certain manufacturing sectors. Western Europe, too, is experiencing some success in the high-technology market, although Europe continues to be plagued by a number of problems that constitute a considerable barrier to effective competition.

The United States still remains the world's leading scientific power, spending approximately $120 billion in 1987, or half of the West's total investment, in research and development.[26] Nevertheless, the U.S. lead in several high-technology areas has disappeared, and it has seen its traditional overall high-technology leadership position decline. For example, in 1986, for the first time, the United States experienced a trade deficit (of $2 billion) in high-technology products (see figure 1), a trend that marked a decline from a $27 billion surplus in 1980.

The causes of this relative decline in the United States are the subject of intense debate. Many see it as a result of unfair trading practices on the part of U.S. allies. Others place the blame on the excessive restrictions on technology transfer imposed because of concern for national security. The most important reason, however, is the heightened capabilities of U.S. competitors.

Japan, in particular, is catching up. Although the Unit-

FIGURE 1
U.S. High-Technology Exports and Imports
(Billion $, Year end)

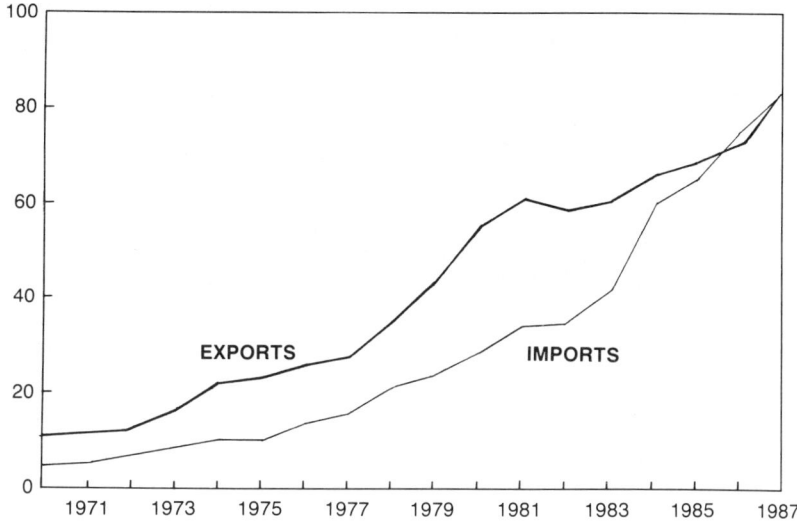

Sources: U.S. Department of Commerce; National Science Foundation.

ed States may still have the largest share of the high-technology market, Japan became the second largest supplier in 1980. Only in communications and electronics, office automation, and ordnance has the United States increased its market share.[27] Japan now leads the world in such areas as gallium arsenide computer chips, robotics and other computer-controlled machine tools, and magnetic storage media.

Japan has built its success, however, not on scientific innovation, but on developing the ideas of others in ways that have enormous commercial appeal. Its strategy was based on licensing a technology and then entering a market with a better product. Through 1986, Japan had won only four Nobel Prizes in science, compared with 158 for the United States.[28]

The problem of Japan's marginal contribution to fundamental scientific breakthroughs and its shortcomings in scientific creativity was underlined by Susumu Tonegawa, a Nobel Prize-winning immunologist now at MIT, who criticized the Japanese research system for stressing conformity at the expense of imaginative boldness that comes from individual research. This view was reinforced by Leo Esaki of IBM, a Nobel winner in physics, who argues that "generally the Japanese are uncomfortable with abstract concepts. . . . Since scientific creativity is the most important element in basic research, it comes as no surprise that Japan lags behind. This is not because applied research has received undue emphasis—it is simply that basic research cannot be done."[29]

Japan confronts other long-term problems including a limited ability in complex systems integration, relatively poor performance in software as well as in upstream mathematical reflection, and the "quasi absence of military R&D (with its need for extreme specifications and corresponding leap-frog effects)."[30]

Despite these problems there is no doubt that Japan will continue as a high-technology powerhouse. This is sure to lead to some friction with the United States. At the same time, there is a growing cooperation and interdependence between the two countries that makes such friction extremely counterproductive. Japan specialist Ellen Frost, for example, believes that the two financial and commercial systems are so intertwined that it would be virtually impossible for there to be a breakdown of the global economy into separate blocs led by the United States and Japan.[31] Indeed, Sheridan Tatsumo argues that the United States and Japan already jointly oversee a complementary technological empire he has described as a "technopolis."[32]

The situation for Europe differs in both its problems and its prospects. Europe's problem is not science, in which European companies are fully competitive with their allies when measured by articles in scientific journals or Nobel Prizes. In fact, in some areas, such as chemicals and pharmaceuticals, Europe leads the rest of the world. It is in innovation – the system of interrelated activities leading to the relatively widespread availability of civilian and military products – that Europe lags behind the United States and Japan. Europe has been less able to move its scientific inventions from the laboratory to the showroom. The scientific basis of magnetic tape, for example, was developed almost 50 years ago, mostly in Europe. Today, 90 percent of its video recorders are imported from Japan.[33] In many other fields – microelectronics, robotics, pharmaceuticals – the conventional wisdom tends to confuse European scientific capabilities with innovation and efficient production and marketing.

One of the several reasons for Europe's lag is attitudinal or sociological. Unlike their U.S. counterparts, European governments and businesses have traditionally emphasized risk aversion and have not accepted the idea that failure is an undesirable though possible outcome of doing business. Another reason is the fragmentation of the research effort, producing only limited intellectual flow among government, business, and academic research efforts. Restrictive tax laws, relatively low levels of research and development funding, limited numbers of trained personnel, and venture capital shortages are also elements that explain Europe's current problems.

The most serious impediment to Western Europe's technological development, however, has been its failure to create a unified market of continental proportions. In the wake of the arduous task of putting Europe back on its feet economically after World War II, the late 1960s and early 1970s found Europe consolidating its economic gains and redistributing its recent wealth through elaborate social nets. At the same time, the United States and Japan were getting ready for their propulsion into the high-technology age. Instead of forming a European market in reply, European countries took a nationalistic course, and each one erected a barricade to protect national industries. The result was described in a Report for the Commission of the European Communities (EC) as follows:

> The Community has an internal market on a scale similar to those of Japan and the United States, but it has to face the competition of those countries with a market segmented by many barriers and with no common technological strategy: with a few notable exceptions, R&D policies and resources are applied by Member States without any coordination.
>
> The consequences are beginning to show. Since 1972 the annual growth rate in real terms of the production of high technology goods in Europe has not exceeded 5%, while the rate in the United States is 7.6% and in Japan 14%.[34]

Another result has been a high-technology deficit in the EC amounting to $12 billion in 1986.[35]

Recognizing this tremendous shortcoming, Europe has taken several important steps to foster greater cooperation and coordination in high-technology research and development (R&D). The push toward a single market in 1992 accounts for much of the current activity. Even before that move gained momentum, Europe – and the EC in particular—began to pursue new cooperative ventures to overcome the fragmented market blocking high-technology progress.

The EC's "Framework Program" embraces all of its cooperative efforts in R&D. The Framework Program is intended to be a programming tool that will facilitate consultation among EC members on scientific and technical objectives, a guide for steering and planning specific programs, and a tool for accurate financial forecasting to assist in decision making.[36] It is intended to alleviate some of the difficulties shared by EC members in a way that fosters greater synergy among their various scientific and technological programs.

Other cooperative programs that have enjoyed some success under EC auspices are RACE (Research into Advanced Communications Technologies in Europe), which is to provide Europe with the technology base for a broadband European communications system, and BRITE (Basic Research in Industrial Technologies for Europe), aimed at stimulating cooperative, precompetitive R&D in areas not already under investigation in industry. Although both of these programs have had their share of shortcomings, enough progress has been made to encourage the Europeans to continue these cooperative efforts.

The EC's "flagship" cooperative R&D program is ESPRIT (the European Strategic Program for Research in Information Technology), which is intended to promote industrial cooperation in information technology. The first phase of the program, funded at a level of almost $2 billion, concentrated on microelectronics, advanced information processing, and the application of computers to manufacturing and office systems. One example of its success is the mini-supercomputer recently launched by Thorn EMI and the French computer firm Telmat. The computer is reported to have the high-speed performance of a supercomputer at a fraction of the cost. Also involved in its development were the universities of Southampton and Grenoble, as well as the French computer firm Apsis and the Royal Signals and Radar Establishment.[37]

The Sub-committee on Advanced Technology and Technology Transfer for the North Atlantic Assembly (NAA) reports that overall funding for ESPRIT has fallen short of what is needed to meet industry's enthusiastic initial support. Although the program has made some impressive advances, the NAA report also argues that ESPRIT has not yet resulted in the "critical mass" needed to make Europe truly competitive.[38]

Despite its shortcomings, ESPRIT has generally been considered a success in fostering trust between European partners and focusing Europe's technological research in strategically important areas. The next phase of ESPRIT is considered crucial because it is intended to push more in the direction of market exploitation through the creation of large technology integration projects that deliberately seek to bring a range of technologies together.

A non-EC cooperative program that also deserves mention is the French-inspired EUREKA, a market-oriented research effort to develop competitive products in the shortest possible time. Conceived because of concern for the commercial spinoffs that might be derived from the U.S. Strategic Defense Initiative (SDI), by September 1987 EUREKA provided an umbrella for a total of 165 projects with a value of $5.8 billion involving more than 600 firms or research entities from 19 countries.[39] EUREKA, too, is not without its problems, including an absence of agreed strategic objectives, but it has been important in fostering greater European self-confidence in its ability to produce competitive research and development that leads to commercially attractive results.

Another aspect of the drive toward greater European coordination of its high-technology research and development has been industrial initiatives to cooperate. Across Europe's high-technology landscape, firms from different countries are rushing to find partners for large and small programs. In computer development, for example, Siemens of the Federal Republic of Germany (FRG), ICL of the United Kingdom (UK), and Bull of France have established a joint research laboratory in Munich.

In semiconductor research, two European giants — Siemens and Philips of the Netherlands — have begun a collaborative effort on new high-density chips. Recently, their talks on a government-backed development project known as Joint European Semiconductor Silicon (JESSI) have been widened to include SGS-Thompson, the joint Italian-French semiconductor firm created in 1987. The EC reportedly now wants also to bring in other European firms including Britain's Plessey.[40]

According to the *Financial Times*, these and many more ventures signify a change in the intellectual climate in Europe that follows decades of skepticism over the wisdom of joint projects. Indeed, the London paper argues that cooperative ventures have become so fashionable in certain parts of the high-technology sector that they are now the norm rather than the exception, seen virtually as an indicator of a company's determination to expand.[41]

The Sum of the Trends: Competition, Cooperation, Protectionism

The drive toward cooperation in Europe is propelled in part by the fear that Europe will be left behind in the global technology race by a more competitive United States and Japan. It is designed to make European firms more competitive by helping develop both their technologies and their markets. Similar motivations — that is, being competitive and securing access to technology and markets — are driving U.S. and Japanese firms toward cooperative efforts as well. Under the pressure of competition, the Japanese have been spurred to change some of their habits and approaches. Similarly, U.S. companies have pursued technical alliances with both Japanese and European firms to strengthen their corporate positions.

The intensity of the competition, however, has also fostered concern that rather than cooperation, protectionism will become the dominant feature of the future industrial landscape. There is considerable unease, for example, about whether Europe after 1992, when the single market is supposed to be established, will be more open or more closed. There are certainly advocates in the EC for the latter position who argue that if Europe is to strengthen its new pan-European industries, they must be protected. A protective if not protectionist attitude has also intensified in the United States, reflected especially in the United States Congress. The Japanese have been quick to refute accusations that their current trade practices are unfair, but Japan's trading partners want more action than words – especially the United States, with its $60 billion dollar deficit with Japan – and they are continuing the pressure to get Tokyo to dismantle barriers that keep out foreign products.

The industrial landscape, therefore, is in a period of significant flux in light of the EC drive toward a single market, major changes in trading relationships, financial flows, and other aspects of economic activity. What is clear is that the technology environment is, and will continue to be, intensely competitive. On the bright side, the trend toward cooperation is encouraging, especially in light of the factors making collaboration an option of continuing attraction. If not carefully handled, however, competition could foster a more protectionist environment that sparks moves and countermoves motivated by narrow national interests that leave the entire West in a worsened economic condition. Which direction is chosen will depend as much upon the political acumen of business and government leaders as upon their economic insight.

Implications for Defense

In a sense, the remainder of this paper is an exploration of the implications for NATO of this tremendously exciting period of change in the global high-technology environment. First, however, the implications of the trends discussed above for defense in general should be addressed.

*The Impact of Defense Research
and Development*

Although the commercial sphere stands in the forefront of today's technological development, many people have expressed concern that defense-related research and development consumes too high a proportion of overall alliance R&D spending, with the result that the West's general economy is held back. Not only does defense R&D consume enormous financial assets, the argument goes, but many of the West's best minds in a range of scientific fields are engaged in defense-related, hence classified, research. The ultimate impact, the critics contend, will be to slow economic growth, reduce the competitiveness of key industrial sectors in individual alliance countries, and, in the end, impede the defense effort as well. This position with respect to the United Kingdom was articulated in a study by the Science Policy Research Unit at the University of Sussex, which argued that, "if Britain is to break the vicious circle of decline, an important precondition must be a reduction in the relative size of the defence sector and level of military R and D. . . . Britain has got to reorient her technological effort way from the defence sector and towards the civilian markets."[42]

This issue is particularly important for the United States, which spends as much as four times more money on military R&D than all of Western Europe. Indeed, as figure 2 shows, the proportion of overall government R&D consumed by defense-related R&D is significantly greater for the United States than for any of its allies. Moreover, within U.S. defense R&D there has been more "D" than "R" in recent years, with funding of basic research and exploratory development actually declining in real terms by 2.5 percent since 1981. This has occurred despite an overall

FIGURE 2
Government R & D Expenditures on Defense
(% of Total Government R & D) (1986)

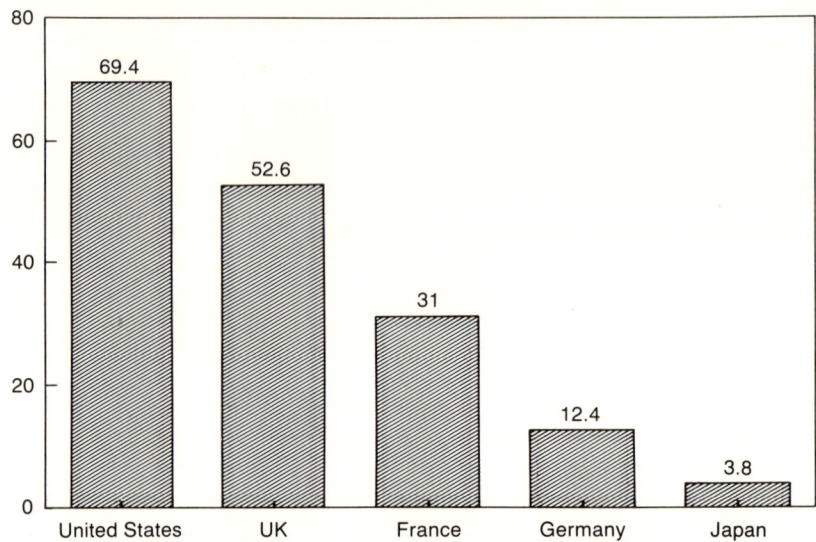

Sources: European Economic Community; Organization for Economic Cooperation and Development; National Science Foundation.

growth in U.S. Research, Development, Test, and Evaluation (RDT&E) of more than 90 percent during the same period.[43]

These trends have provoked some concern about the level of effort devoted to fundamental research, which not only offers long-term military payoffs, but also contains the greatest potential for commercial spinoffs. As one newspaper reported, "there is growing concern among many scientists and engineers that the price of winning the arms race with the Soviet Union is the loss of an equally vital lead in civilian technologies to Japan and other industrialized nations."[44]

The position of the Reagan administration has been that the private sector should be essentially responsible for commercial R&D, and that R&D in the defense sector is aimed at enhancing national security. Commercial spinoffs from defense R&D are welcome but not necessary.

The administration, however, has not been oblivious to the impact of lack of support for basic research. One critical implication, for example, could be excessive dependence upon foreign sources for components that are critical to the performance of advanced weapons systems. This relationship was highlighted by the Defense Science Board study of the growing U.S. dependence in the defense sector on foreign semiconductors. The conclusions of this study prompted the creation of SEMATECH (Semiconductor Manufacturing Technology Institute), a joint DOD–private sector initiative to regain ground the United States has lost in the semiconductor market.

A balance between commercial and defense research and development is obviously necessary. For the United States that balance has been askew. A strong economy is the ultimate prerequisite for a viable military in that the economy provides the resources for the continual development of increasingly advanced military capabilities. To be competitive in the military sphere, a nation must also be competitive commercially.

The Alliance Dimension

What is true for the United States in terms of commercial and military competitiveness is also true for its NATO allies. Many of those allies, however, do not have the same advantages in promoting economic growth as does the United States, if for no other reason than that they are so much smaller. If Europe is successful in creating a single market after 1992, that situation could change dramatically, at least with respect to the size of the market available to European firms. Until that happens, however, NATO's task of implementing an effective technology management strategy – as a coalition – will face a very stiff challenge.

One of NATO's major difficulties is that its members

are operating on at least four – and perhaps more – different levels within the rapidly changing technology environment. The United States is the only NATO member that is a world-class power across the full spectrum of advanced technology. At a second level stand the major European states – Germany, France, the United Kingdom, and increasingly, Italy. These countries have very significant technological capabilities, but they do not span the same range as the United States. The smaller central and northern European countries have an even further restricted scope, although there are some technology giants in those countries, such as Philips in the Netherlands. Finally, there are the states of NATO's southern region that are clearly lagging behind in the advanced technology sector. Some of those countries, Spain and Turkey in particular, have made impressive gains in recent years and demonstrate a commitment to developing their technological base even more rapidly. They continue to suffer, however, from a lack of resources and limited infrastructure.

Given the intense competition in some areas of advanced technology and the wide variation in technological capabilities among allies in others, NATO will have difficulty reconciling different national approaches to exploiting advanced technology in the years ahead, especially because national economic interests are also at stake. Some Europeans have long worried, for example, that because of its technological prowess the United States wants to corner NATO's high-technology market, forcing all other members to buy the most sophisticated – and usually the most expensive – equipment from U.S. firms.

In view of these difficulties, how can a mutually acceptable balance of transatlantic defense technology trade be achieved, especially one that meets NATO's needs on the battlefield? What are the advanced technologies that everyone must have, and can every ally handle them? Can the allies buy them in adequate numbers, considering the high cost of advanced technology? How does NATO bridge the gap in the technological sophistication of the United States and some European states on one hand, and the nations of the southern region on the other? How can NATO nations work together to lessen that technological imbalance and get technology into the field in the most usable, timely, and cost effective manner?

The rapidly changing global technology environment is making the answer to all of these questions more difficult. The speed of that change, its scope and complexity, the impact in the industrial sector, and heightened competitiveness are only some of the factors that will affect NATO's search for solutions. NATO policymakers face a daunting task indeed. Their starting point, however, must be the best possible understanding of what new technology is making possible on the battlefield. Equally necessary is a clear understanding of how technology relates to other aspects of conflict that will be as critical – if not more so – in determining its outcome.

2

Technology's Impact on Future Battlefields[1]

THE CASE STUDY: FOLLOW-ON FORCES ATTACK

On November 9, 1984, NATO's Defense Planning Committee formally approved the Supreme Allied Commander Europe's (SACEUR's) Long-Term Planning Guideline for Follow-On Forces Attack (FOFA), making the concept an official part of NATO's approach to a possible conventional conflict in Europe. FOFA had its origins in SACEUR's concern over the prospects for NATO's success in the conventional phase in a European conflict, and the planning guideline was recognition by alliance political authorities that action had to be taken. When first introduced, FOFA met with some opposition, especially in Europe, on political, operational, and economic grounds—opposition that has become less intense over time. The FOFA concept, which basically calls for attack against targets in the enemy's rear areas, relies heavily on a range of high technologies currently under development or proposed by several alliance members. As a consequence, it represents a good case study of the way that advanced technology could shape the battlefield of the future—the issue at the core of any NATO technology management strategy.

According to a study of FOFA by the congressional Office of Technology Assessment, "the purpose of attacking follow-on forces is to impede the ability of the Warsaw Pact commanders to bring their ground forces into the battle when they want to and at full strength." In simple terms it means using longer-range weapons—whether artillery, rocket launchers, aircraft, or missiles—to "delay, disrupt, and destroy" enemy forces that have not yet engaged NATO in direct combat. This objective is worth making a high priority given NATO's analysis of the importance of Soviet reinforcements to the success of the Warsaw Pact's concept of conventional military operations.

Several factors came together simultaneously to produce the FOFA concept and get it adopted by the allies, despite some initial reservations. First, the analysis of the Soviet approach to conflict suggested that attacking follow-on forces could pay a significant dividend. Second, both military and political decision makers in NATO recognized that no NATO nation would be able to generate meaningful numbers of new forces to meet the increasing challenge in the continuing Soviet build-up of its conventional forces; consequently, attention was focused on technology for possible force multipliers. Third, interdiction, that is, striking targets in the enemy's rear area to impede the forward movement of reinforcements, has been a traditional NATO mission, but new technologies producing more accurate and lethal weapons systems were expanding the possible scope of such action and making new options available.

Although FOFA was developed by the Supreme Headquarters Allied Powers Europe (SHAPE), the concept also had an inescapable link to new concepts that were being developed by the U.S. Army and Air Force at about the same time. The U.S. Army concepts, some of which came to be integrated into a concept labeled "AirLand Battle," called as well for deep fire, primarily as part of an effort to break up the enemy's offensive, but also to restore the initiative to U.S. forces. Although there is a link, SACEUR has been very careful to distinguish between AirLand Battle and FOFA, arguing that the former is the U.S. Army doctrine for worldwide conflict and not necessarily appropriate for the NATO area in all its particulars, while promoting the latter as the agreed NATO approach.

FOFA has many different possible concepts of operation involving different weapons and attack schemes. These can range from artillery attack of armored columns as close to the front as 5 kilometers or as far away as 30, to attack by aircraft against choke points such as bridges 150 kilometers to the rear, to missile attack against rail networks as far from the front as 800 kilometers. Whatever the concept, however, a FOFA operation must include the functions of reconnaissance, surveillance, situation assessment, target acquisition, weapons delivery, target kill, and attack control. Obviously, no one system can perform all of these tasks, and the concept can only be implemented effectively through the integration of a number of different systems. These systems would include reconnaissance, surveillance and target acquisition (RSTA) capabilities, attack platforms, munitions and submunitions, and a command and control (C^2) network. This trend toward the performance of missions by "packages" or "systems of systems" is one of the most significant developments for the battlefield of the future.

None of the FOFA concepts could be fully implemented today because all of the necessary technology is not yet available. NATO'S current ability to attack rear targets, for example, is inherent almost exclusively in aircraft with a range of only 150 kilometers armed with weapons most effective against stationary targets, not the moving armored columns envisioned in the more elaborate versions of FOFA. NATO's most severe shortcomings can be found in RSTA and C^2 systems that do not provide timely information on moving targets, a shortage of attack platforms other than aircraft, and munitions limited in both capability and number.

Of course, systems are already being planned to address some of these shortcomings. In the RSTA area, for example, the Joint Surveillance Target Attack Radar System (JSTARS) is being designed to look over wide areas for long periods of time to find moving targets and report that information to users in a matter of seconds. Unfortunately, the program has run into difficulty in the Congress. Attention is also being given to the contribution of unmanned aerial vehicles for RSTA. Regarding attack platforms, the Army Tactical Missile System (ATACMS) is a ballistic missile designed to be fired out of a Multiple Launch Rocket System (MLRS) with a range of more than 100 kilometers and great accuracy. Scatterable mines, sensor-fused weapons designed to be accurate and effective especially against tanks, and top-attack weapons also for use against tanks are the greatest area of exploration in the munitions area.

One of the initial worries about FOFA was that it depended too heavily on technology that was not yet available or that would be overly complex. Critics cited numerous cases when a heralded weapons system never made it to the battlefield because it did not perform up to specifications or became too expensive. They worried that the same thing could happen to some of the systems, such as JSTARS, that were seen to be key to FOFA operations.

Europeans also expressed concern that most of the advanced technology being touted for FOFA was American. Was FOFA just another way to force the Europeans to "buy American," ensuring that the United States would remain the alliance leader in military technology? Through a U.S. DOD Defense Science Board Task Force on FOFA and the 1985 Nunn-Roth-Warner cooperative research and development amendment, the United States has been trying to allay these alliance concerns and pursue more FOFA programs on a joint basis. At this point, the Europeans appear most interested in FOFA systems that will enhance the performance of systems they already have in the field, such as the Tornado aircraft, and they show little enthusiasm for systems such as ATACMS that extend the FOFA capability to longer ranges.

It was not only technology that prompted European concerns about FOFA, however. Some Europeans argued that by stressing the attack of forces deep in the enemy rear, the concept was overly offensive and inconsistent with NATO's commitment to defense. This criticism was especially strong from the European Left, which emphasized FOFA's relationship to AirLand Battle, and which worried that the concept would serve as a barrier to any effective arms control by fueling a new aspect of the arms race. The European Left also argued that FOFA, especially in its more elaborate versions, would be destabilizing because its planned use of tactical ballistic missiles to conduct conventional operations would be indistinguishable from the nuclear versions of such weapons.

On the military level, concern was raised that giving priority to FOFA would draw attention and resources away from ensuring that the first echelon of Warsaw Pact forces could be stopped. This requirement was seen by some in Europe as much more critical, because, if the initial defense collapsed, there would be no need to "strike deep" because the war would be all but over. In essence, those who took this position argued that FOFA was the wrong priority. In part to ameliorate the concern that NATO was not paying adequate attention to front-line defense, alliance decision makers listed both successful defense against Warsaw Pact first echelon forces and striking deep as two key mission components of allied forces in its first version of the 1985 Conceptual Military Framework (CMF). The CMF was developed by alliance military authorities at the request of the political leadership to provide a planning framework for the alliance, looking 20, rather than NATO's traditional 5 or 6, years ahead.

Despite these reservations, with the adoption of FOFA as a Long-Term Planning Guideline, NATO committed itself to incorporating the concept into its operational planning. It is too early to determine, however, how the "operationalization" of FOFA will be balanced by alliance policymakers against the other important tasks that must be accomplished by NATO's conventional forces, especially at a time when resources will be increasingly scarce.

Nevertheless, FOFA remains a major new development in the alliance. The Follow-on Forces Attack concept demonstrates that new technologies can create opportunities for innovative operational concepts, revised doctrines, and improved tactics that will help make NATO's strategy of flexible response more flexible and, hence, more effective. It also shows that technological change can make possible certain things that military commanders have long desired to do but have not had the capability to implement. Most important perhaps, FOFA demonstrates that the application of the wide diversity of available new technology to the battlefield of the future will be extremely complicated. The chances for serious mistakes are good if careful attention is not paid to the integration of technology on the battlefield. This is true not only with regard to the integration of various technologies themselves, but also with regard to the integration of technology and other critical aspects such as manpower and logistics. Those complications and relationships are the subjects of this chapter.

Introduction

Technology's contribution to conventional warfare has markedly—some might say conclusively—increased in modern times. One defense analyst has argued, for example, that "if Clausewitz' trinity [of the people, government, and the military] is indeed both unchanged and changeless, technology must be the additional factor required for our understanding of contemporary and future warfare. Without it we will fail to see the new problems and opportunities that it may present."[2] Faced with such importance, and awed by what modern technology can accomplish, we risk becoming technology "junkies" with an unholy faith in a technological answer to winning the next war. The German Panzers demonstrated in 1940, however, that technology will make a difference only when there is the force structure, command philosophy, operational concepts, tactics, and communications necessary to exploit the possibilities it creates.

Unlike past periods of history when technological and tactical change have been long in coming, the unprecedented rate at which technology develops today represents a profound challenge to NATO policymakers who must decide how and with what weapons the alliance will fight. If the effective integration of technology and tactics has been the key to past battlefield success, can the already demanding process of integration meet the increasing challenges posed by the remarkably rapid rate of contemporary technological change? Can conceptual and operational innovations keep pace with the technological explosion? How can NATO ensure that technological advantage will be translated expeditiously from the laboratory to the battlefield?

Alliance decision makers confront these difficult questions at a time when, as military historian Michael Handel argues, "the gap that has opened up between the birth of new technology and its proper absorption into military doctrine and practice is likely to be permanent."[3] Handel probably overstates the case; the problem is not new. Appropriate operational modifications to technological change have often been resisted and slow in coming.[4] As Handel himself points out, in World War II "weapons and doctrine, technology and its intellectual understanding were rarely in harmony."[5]

Today, the problem is further complicated because the growing complexity of both current technology and modern warfare makes it difficult for anyone, civilian or military, to have the necessary knowledge in all the requisite areas. With few exceptions, political leaders have little detailed understanding of military technology. Many military people are technicians with specific knowledge of individual systems but are insufficiently trained in operations and strategy.

Moreover, there are few crucibles in which to test new ideas. In the past, colonial wars or limited conflicts provided the opportunity to explore new ideas made possible by technological innovations. Those testing grounds do not exist today. It is true that the U.S. war in Vietnam and the Soviet Union's conflict in Afghanistan generated new operational and tactical ideas (in the use of helicopters, for example). They also served as a testing ground for new technology (the Soviets' "liquid fire" for use against runways, for example). Those conflicts in no way resemble the kind of battlefield that would exist in central Europe if deterrence failed, however, and there is no other place in the world where such a conflict could be replicated.

The importance of finding answers to the question of technology's impact on the course of future conflict is obvious. Western nations have traditionally emphasized technological development as a fundamental dimension of successful achievement—promoting continuing economic growth and prosperity, fostering a constantly improving quality of life, and providing an important contribution to the successful prosecution of conflict. Indeed, in war, technology is a profound force multiplier.

Today, however, that impact does not come without high cost. The ever increasing cost of advanced technology makes it the target of policymakers' cuts in a period of severely constrained government spending throughout the West. The explosion of technological advances gives defense planners an enormous menu from which to choose. But choose they must, and the combination of innumerable options and limited resources demands that great care be given to putting money on technological horses that can go the distance with the greatest payoff on the battlefield.

The tough technological choices confronting Western policymakers go beyond which technologies are critical to how those technologies should be applied. If the United States and its allies are to implement fully the opportunities new technology creates, they must first decide the ways in which it can be most useful. This is not an easy decision because it often becomes ensnared in the bureaucratic brier patches of defense budget debates. New platforms incorporating the latest technological advances, for example, have powerful lobbies because they absorb large resources. These programs, in turn, translate into jobs in congressional districts and budgetary preeminence in intraservice battles. Using that same technology to upgrade existing platforms or equip them with more advanced munitions is much less glamorous, but it may prove to be more cost effective.

Similarly, the broader context of conflict in which technology is applied and utilized will shape its ultimate effectiveness, and a proper understanding of that context is critical to ensure the maximum impact of any given technology. Of greatest importance in this regard is understanding that, despite the mechanization of virtually all aspects of warfare over the last century, war remains a quintessentially human activity. If one ever forgets the human dimensions of conflict, all the technology in the world is unlikely to prevent final defeat.

Alan Gropman, a former air force officer and current defense industry executive, provides an excellent example of keeping the human dimension paramount, drawing on the man-machine interface, which is one aspect of the human quality of war.[6] He points out that for aviators, air superiority is largely a function of technology, and aviators' morale is seriously depressed when they lose confidence in their airplanes. One might extend Gropman's point to the infantryman and his rifle, the artillery officer and his cannon, or the air defense battery crew and its missile. The impact of technology on the intangible of morale may ultimately have more to do with success or failure on the battlefield than how far that technology has actually advanced.

The Need For Trade-offs

It is in this broader context that NATO must consider its choices about which technologies to pursue and how to apply them. The question alliance policymakers must answer has been posed by RAND analyst Ben Lambeth: "Across what performance spectrum, in what force mix, numerical strength, and sustainability do we need to give us our desired mission effectiveness for most plausible scenarios at a cost we can afford?"[7]

Inherent in Lambeth's question is a series of trade-offs

NATO policymakers must address. First, *quality vs. quantity*. The extremely high cost of contemporary high technology represents a significant opportunity cost. Higher and higher costs have translated into fewer and fewer, albeit more capable, systems on the battlefield. Yet, a point is reached at which the opportunity costs become important. The Belgian decision not to purchase the Patriot air defense system, for example, was a budgetary, not a military one. The impact has been to complicate an already difficult air defense problem not just for the Belgian corps but for all alliance forces in Germany.

Second, *high-tech vs. low-tech*. No member of NATO, including the United States, can afford a purely "high-tech" military structure. The choice is really one of the mix of the advanced and less advanced technologies incorporated into the force structure and how they will be used together. There has been a tendency, for example, to marry high-technology platforms and high-technology weapons. In a period of constrained resources, this approach may not prove to be the best way to utilize limited resources fully. Smart weapons matched with "dumb" platforms (such as drones or remotely piloted vehicles), for example, might be more appropriate.

Third, *today's threat vs. tomorrow's*. Should NATO emphasize "the new" or "the improved"? Current decisions regarding the introduction of advanced technology systems will mean those systems will not enter the inventory for 10 years at least. The Soviet Union, however, is fielding equipment today that makes the current NATO inventory less effective. Should current technology be used, then, to promote fundamental improvements in force performance by fostering basic change or change at the margin? How much redesign of systems is needed to optimize the impact of newly available or prospective technologies, especially ones that are likely to be very expensive?

NATO policymakers confront the trade-off between upgrading existing equipment that can be fielded more rapidly against the ongoing Soviet buildup or waiting until the next generation of weapons enters the inventory, with all of the implications delay entails. As IISS Director François Heisbourg has pointed out, "an excess of technical ambition runs high risks."[8] The military services have confronted the question with respect to low observable, or "stealth," technology. Although the technology promises a major payoff, it is coming at an enormous cost that forecloses pursuit of other opportunities.

Upgrades could provide significant enhancement of existing systems. Upgrade packages for the M113 armored personnel carrier or the attack helicopter are two examples. At the same time, these are not inexpensive, either. For example, to counteract a widening gap between U.S. and Soviet armored forces, the Senate Armed Services Committee voted almost $100 million for urgent upgrades of antiarmor weapons and U.S. tanks, while the House Armed Services Committee voted to add $260 million.[9] That money is not available, then, for investment in development of more advanced systems. There is clearly a heightened interest in upgrades. The effort to produce the Agile Falcon and the Hornet 2000 before the Advanced Technology Fighter is available may be a harbinger of the future.

A complementary approach, increasing in popularity, is to direct force procurements to prolong the life of existing platforms through technological improvements of the things they carry. This would mean fewer points in time — and longer spans between them — when major new systems are introduced.

Finally, *high technology vs. readiness and sustainability*. In NATO today, most member states have not achieved their stated goal of 30-day stocks of critical ammunition. In the minds of many, such as former SACEUR General Bernard Rogers, this shortage of ammunition is NATO's single most glaring weakness. Unfortunately, during the budgeting process, ammunition has little appeal and a small constituency compared with the advocates of advanced and expensive platforms and electronics. The option of delaying new equipment acquisitions in favor of accelerated ammunition purchases is not one that policy-makers find attractive, but it is one that they may be forced to accept.

It may be that the traditional contrast between high technology, on the one hand, and readiness and sustainability, on the other, will actually diminish. This would result from the use of high technology to increase reliability and, as defense analyst David Hobbs puts it, "ease of maintenance." Specifications for the Advanced Tactical Fighter (ATF), for example, demand reliability and reductions in maintenance and support burdens.

Revolution or Evolution?

Is the impact of technological change on the battlefield evolutionary or revolutionary? The question, of course, is impossible to answer without qualification. Does it mean, for example, the impact of one specific technological change or in only one area of technology? If so, then its impact is evolutionary. Even the enormous advances in electronics are basically exploited to help do better the basic tasks of the armed forces, whether it is communicating commands, delivering weapons on targets, or maneuvering for protection. In and of themselves, most individual technologies have not opened up wholly new activities that might determine the course of conflict.

If one poses the initial question in terms of the sum of technological change, however, then a different answer is possible. Taken together, the technological changes that will be incorporated into the battlefields of the future are likely to force major alterations in the organization, doctrines, and operational techniques of all military forces. The opening up of space from which more and more of the earth can be seen, for example, presents fundamental challenges for the navy, which has traditionally used the vast expanses of the ocean for concealment and protection.

The requirements that new systems are designed to

meet are a further consideration in assessing the general impact of new technology. How narrowly or broadly will those requirements be defined? Naval analyst Norman Friedman argues, in the case of the navy at least, that specialized requirements will become too costly to pursue:

> In principle, the Third World mission could be carried out by a specialized and distinct naval force, but in practice that is probably unaffordable. Thus national strategy imposes a sort of boundary condition on acceptable naval strategy: the same fleet must be usable both in global . . . and in local and limited war. That condition in turn should affect the balance of investment within the navy.[10]

Although NATO does not have to confront Third World missions, it nevertheless confronts the same type of limitation because too restrictive definitions of systems requirements will be unaffordable. A necessary flexibility in its forces will be a major factor in determining which systems are chosen and what technology they will incorporate. Friedman contends, for example, that the air force is beginning to share the navy's experience of depending on platforms that are so expensive that, once destroyed, they are not easily replaced.[11] Such a situation leads to a growing reluctance to put those expensive platforms at risk. This translates in turn into finding new ways to perform assigned tasks, that is, new requirements that are broad enough that the same expensive platform can be used to fulfill a number of needs.

The issue of defining requirements raises the additional question of the relationship between strategy and technology. Clearly, technology must be placed in a strategic context, for strategy — how the forces will be used — will be a major modifier of purely numerical and technological force balances such as that existing between NATO and the Warsaw Pact.[12] Strategic choice will define the organization and operation of military forces and establish the channels for the development and application of new technology. There is no way to avoid such channeling, but what must be avoided, at all costs, is the development of an inflexible attitude that neither allows the creation of new channels if technological advances suggest novel possibilities nor fosters an ability to react quickly to new developments. The Israelis, for example, may not have anticipated the threat precision-guided weapons posed to tank operations in the 1973 war, but they were quickly able to devise successful countermeasures.[13]

New Military Technologies: What Will They Do?

When looking in more detail at the impact of new technology on battlefields of the future, it is not especially useful to break down the analysis into traditional land, sea, air, and space dimensions. Rather, one must look at the functional aspects of the battle to determine where technology can have its biggest payoff. The following brief survey is not meant to be comprehensive in discussing every technology now under development in the alliance; rather, it is intended to highlight some of those technologies and their potential impact to convey a sense of the kinds of decisions confronting NATO policymakers.[14]

Reconnaissance, Surveillance,
and Target Acquisition

It can be argued that technological advances in RSTA have been monumental, if not revolutionary. The major change has been to extend reconnaissance and surveillance beyond the traditional limits of visual or radar sensing. Today, what the battlefield commander can see spreads much deeper, far beyond the line of sight; it is not shrouded by fog or night, and it is much more precisely defined because greater discrimination exists regarding what is on the battlefield. The range of seismic, thermal, magnetic, or acoustic devices currently used and projected increasingly can distinguish between tanks and trucks, radar installations and air defense locations, and so on.[15] The importance of this growing capability is enormous because on the battlefields of the future, whoever shoots first has a distinct advantage, and shooting first depends on finding targets first.

The current trend in RSTA technology is expected to continue, enhancing capabilities still further. Systems such as JSTARS will look even deeper and more discriminately across the battlefield. They will be able to spot moving targets far behind front lines, plot their speed and direction, and adjust attacks against them by air, missile, artillery, or some combination. Other alliance nations are also developing airborne battlefield surveillance systems. Although extremely useful, for the most part they will not offer JSTARS capability. The British ASTOR and French ORCHIDEE are two examples.

More widespread use of longer-range, remotely piloted vehicles (RPVs) will introduce even greater versatility. The U.S. Aquila program was the most ambitious, but it encountered development difficulties and was canceled in the FY 89 budget, although the Congress left some money in the budget to continue an RPV program embracing a family of systems. The U.S. DARPA is also exploring the concept of an unmanned aerial vehicle (UAV) that can fly for days at very high altitudes observing and tracking enemy targets for future attacks. The Amber reconnaissance vehicle is a winged, propeller-driven craft that has been flown continuously for 31 hours at altitudes as high as 23,000 feet.[16]

The British are also pushing ahead with their Phoenix RPV program, as is the FRG with the Toucan. Canada, France, Italy, and Greece are also developing unmanned aerial vehicles of various types.

There are several implications in these trends. First, they promise to diminish greatly the uncertainty confronting a battlefield commander regarding enemy dispositions and intentions. Reducing that uncertainty is one of a commander's highest objectives. If Napoleon had been aware of Field Marshall Gebhard Blucher's movements prior to and during the battle of Waterloo, the outcome of that "near run thing" might have been far different.

Some analysts suggest, however, that new RSTA assets will inundate command positions with information, making it difficult to determine what is truly important and what is not. Another result might be so to slow the ability to process raw data into a usable form that its potentially positive impact is lost. John Macrostie argues that although information overload might be a problem, "a far worse condition than too much information . . . is not enough information."[17] Technology itself might help to resolve this dilemma with the application of artificial intelligence to help select and package the most important of all the available information.

Another impact of expanding RSTA capabilities is increased dependence on nonorganic sensors and the integration of "systems of systems." Such a shift is especially important, as Admiral William Small has argued, in a more "stealthy" environment where the maxim will be that any platform that depends on its own sensors and weapons for mission success can be defeated by a less observable opponent.[18] FOFA is a good example of this trend because it clearly demonstrates that a package of systems, including RSTA, platforms, munitions, and command and control, is required to strike targets successfully in the enemy's rear areas or across operational boundaries, and no single component will prove fully useful without the others.

An important implication of this trend is budgetary. Considering the integration of systems that is increasingly required, budgetary decisions about respective systems should be made on a "package of systems" basis rather than on the individual line items basis that is currently in use by the U.S. Congress. With the present approach, chances are increased that a key system in the package could be eliminated for reasons unrelated to its performance without proper appreciation of its necessity to the entire package.

Firepower

Improvements in weapons accuracy are such that whoever fires first gains a significant advantage, and firing first presupposes being the first to acquire the target. This is done by not only seeing him first, but hitting him first. The most significant trend in firepower, therefore, is the extended range at which targets are engaged. The combination of RSTA improvements and missile technology in particular has smashed the traditional constraints on firepower that have limited the ability to fire beyond what a gunner could see.

Several implications derive from this trend. First, indirect fire systems will continue to increase in importance, not least because of their expanded capabilities against hardened targets. This widening appeal is principally the result of the combination of increased use of multiple submunitions and terminal guidance (as in Copperhead). As a result, there is heightened interest in longer-range close combat systems such as the Fiber Optic Guided Missile (FOG-M) and Long-Range Antitank (LRAT) weapon.[19] The fiber optics of the FOG-M, for example, would eliminate the need to locate expensive and complex electronics in the missile itself, making the system cheaper and more reliable. Its range and, more important, the survivability it offers firing units (because it does not need line-of-sight guidance) are considered especially attractive features.[20]

Long-range fire support systems—Copperhead, Hellfire, SADARM (Sense and Destroy Armored), and SKEET—are also receiving considerable attention. This trend could also intensify the push for deployment of autonomous unmanned systems such as the Tacit Rainbow antiradar attack system, especially if they incorporate stealth technology.

Second, extended firepower range raises questions about the relationship between platforms and weapons. It is cheaper to modify rather than replace platforms—whether tanks, ships, or airplanes—and it is better yet to modify the weapons those platforms carry. Such a philosophy, however, runs counter to army, navy, and air force thinking, which often favors platforms in times of austerity. Nevertheless, what a platform carries (weapons, munitions, sensors, and so forth) increasingly will determine the ultimate effectiveness of the entire system. A tank with a shorter-range gun, for example, no matter how good it is in other ways, would have problems against a gun with a longer range. This relationship and the desire to protect platforms clearly explain the heightened interest in standoff technology that promises greater accuracy at even longer ranges than currently enjoyed.

Third, the growing emphasis on standoff technology and deep attack could have important operational implications. These capabilities need not be directed at the enemy rear; they will also have a major impact if fired laterally across the front. It is this cross-boundary capability as much as the capability for deep attack that makes these systems attractive, and it has led some analysts to suggest that they can be used in ways similar to mobile reserves.[21]

If this proves to be the case, the impact could be enormous. In central Europe, operational reserves are critical, but NATO nations confront the prospect of serious manpower shortages that could force cuts in front-line forces or those reserves. If some technologies provide even a partial way out of this dilemma, they could well represent important areas for investment.

Fourth, extended firepower ranges and other technological advances are enhancing the role of artillery. Almost 60 percent of all battle casualties in World War II were caused by artillery.[22] Nevertheless, after the war artillery rather fell out of favor. In the 1990s, improved weapons in terms of range, accuracy, area of coverage, and the ability to engage multiple targets represent an appealing flexibility to commanders. The terminally guided Phase III MLRS is a case in point. The MLRS can provide high-volume area fire support, counterbattery fire, or air defense suppression. It can be used to scatter mines. MLRS launchers will also be used to launch the ATACMS equipped with 16 to 24 terminally guided submunitions.

Two other aspects of technological change in battlefield firepower that must be mentioned are the new forms being explored and the impact of automation. Regarding new systems, two in particular that offer interesting possibilities are the electromagnetic gun and battlefield lasers. The capabilities of electrically powered guns, including extended ranges, stem from high-projectile speeds achieved by their nonexplosive projectiles — up to six kilometers per second.[23] The problem with such guns is the need to develop small but substantial power supplies to replace the very large packages now needed.[24] Advocates of such systems argue that if this obstacle can be overcome, the electromagnetic gun represents an enhanced system against both tanks and helicopters.

Low-powered lasers are already used extensively on the battlefield, primarily for range finding and target acquisition. If these lasers can be made more powerful, they, too, could extend the range of current systems with far greater accuracy. Preliminary research in the Federal Republic of Germany suggests that such weapons could be especially helpful against airborne targets after the turn of the century.[25]

Finally, some consideration must be given to the possibility of greater automation on the battlefield through a combination of robotics and artificial intelligence. Several prototypes for the land battle have already been produced, such as the Teleoperated Mobile Antiarmor Platform, a four-wheeled vehicle armed with four antitank missiles and a machine gun that can be directed by an operator up to four kilometers away.[26]

Some might think that such trends could lead to replacing people on the battlefield with machines. To the extent that the introduction of robots will relieve manpower pressures, they are to be welcomed. It is highly unlikely, however, that war will ever be fully automated and that people will be eliminated. That is both a strength and a weakness. Human involvement ensures that conflict will be guided and controlled. On the other hand, the man-machine interface represents a point of vulnerability that can always be attacked. Moreover, the number of tasks that robots might perform is likely to remain relatively limited for some time. In the naval area, for example, small robot submarines could become a possibility, but they certainly cannot automate an aircraft carrier! While robotics is important, therefore, caution must be used in assessing the ultimate impact of automation.

Command, Control, and Communications

The explosion of RSTA capabilities will impose daunting command, control, and communications (C^3) demands. As John Macrostie points out, "the need is apparent in all battle scenarios—high and low intensity conflict—on the offense or the defense, and in all geographic areas—be it Western Europe, the Mideast or Korea."[27] The postwar five-fold increase in command personnel in most Western armies reflects this heightened burden.[28]

Command has been described as the glue that holds a modern ground force together; its function is to coordinate the interaction between RSTA systems and combat units.[29] It is also the capability that makes combined arms or integrated operations possible. This is no easy task on the modern battlefield, where the separate communication channels for the functions of combat—maneuver, logistics, fire support, air defense, and so forth—must be coordinated for success.

Advances in microelectronics in particular have given battlefield commanders the ability to integrate incoming data and to transmit a more complex picture back to field commanders for action. Through this growing capability, the commander can more easily establish priorities and use his assets most effectively. Data fusion and battle management are increasingly integrated and will become even more so with systems such as the Joint Tactical Fusion Program

(JTFP) and the Joint Tactical Information Distribution System (JTIDS). A pilot, for example, could use JTIDS to furnish information on missile battery sites, recovery bases, and the location of hostile and friendly forces, both air and ground. These capabilities are only likely to increase with the current investment in VHSIC, superconductivity, and artificial intelligence.

The ability given to a commander by new C³ systems to influence the battle over an expanded battlefield is offset by several factors. First, the battlefield will be much more complex. Therefore, while C³ abilities will increase, the demands placed on command and control will also be heavier. Commanders and their staffs will have to be much better prepared to handle vastly increased quantities of data.

This increased demand will also impose great burdens on the design of C³ systems themselves. The software involved is enormously complex. During the 1970s, for example, the United States failed in its effort to develop a system embracing the battlefield and theater command and control of the army, navy, and air force. As a result, the United States was forced to buy the French RITA system (in the largest single foreign purchase ever by the U.S. military at more than $4 billion), which itself took France and Belgium more than 15 years to develop.[30]

Second, there is tension between the centralization that new C³ fosters at higher levels of command and the decentralization that will characterize certain aspects of future battlefields. On the one hand, former Supreme Allied Commander Atlantic (SACLANT) Admiral Harry Train has pointed out that, with new C³ technologies, nations have created a command and control loop by means of which they exercise the "two thousand mile screwdriver," adjusting a political-military vernier at the scene of an engagement.[31] On the other hand, some analysts argue that future battlefields will be characterized by separate units fighting smaller, independent battles.[32] If this proves to be so, it will further contribute to the battlefield's complexity, imposing even greater demands on the C³ system.

Third, the C³ system is vulnerable. Despite immense progress made in creating multiple forms of communication, improving jam resistance, and hardening, countermeasures are being explored, especially microwave technologies. Another area of possible vulnerability is the current dependence of all military forces on communication satellites. That dependence will only increase. The argument has been made that great strategic leverage could be gained by deploying weapons in space that would target these critical platforms. As a result, pressure could grow to introduce antisatellite weapon (ASAT) systems despite efforts to ban them.[33]

Finally, C³ will be complicated by the alliance context of a conflict involving NATO. The growing lack of C³ interoperability is an area of great concern to NATO commanders. If several allies continue their independent pursuit of C³ technological opportunities, that problem will only worsen. On the tactical level, for example, NATO nations are increasingly unable to talk with one another because they have developed their own advanced field radios with little if any reference to one another's programs. This suggests that much greater alliance attention must be paid to coordination of C³ procurement.

Survivability

To survive on the battlefield requires mobility, concealment, and protection, or some combination of the three. Technological advances made in these areas could be some of the most critical factors shaping the battlefield of the future.

Mobility and Maneuver

Mobility will be absolutely essential for future military forces of all kinds. Tactical mobility will be especially critical. For this reason, NATO countries are exploring a variety of technological options to move forces on the battlefield.

The U.S. M1 Block II, for example, is expected to have a more powerful turbine engine and power train for the next generation of main battle tank. The new French LeClerc tank reportedly will achieve a top speed of 75 kilometers per hour.[34] Use of helicopters to provide necessary movement of forces on the battlefield is another area continuing to be explored through such programs as the U.S. LHX and Franco-German joint helicopter programs, despite the problems they have both encountered.

Mobility is also being emphasized for other battlefield systems. By reducing the crew size and combining all the components in one vehicle, the Firefinder II radar system, which will be used with the MLRS and the HIP howitzer, can reduce emplacement and displacement times by about 80 percent.[35]

Both offense and defense must move to achieve their objectives. Movement, however, attracts attention, and attention invites destruction. As a consequence, although movement remains essential, it has also become more dangerous. All forces will be affected, whether forward forces concentrating for an initial attack, reserve forces shifting to exploit opportunities or reinforcing a flagging effort, or defensive forces counterattacking to blunt an enemy's penetration.

Whether this change will ultimately favor the offense or defense cannot be answered by looking at technology alone. Defense analyst Daniel Kaufmann reminds us that other, perhaps decisive, factors will also come into play—strategic and tactical surprise, operational sophistication, tactical skill, and the shock effect of modern weapons. Because both offense and defense are subject to the dangers inherent in concentration and maneuver, the result could be an extended war of attrition, at least until stockpiles of modern munitions are depleted.[36]

In the air war, the issue is maneuverability rather than mobility. Although the major trend is toward beyond-visual-range weapons and sensors, some U.S. government researchers estimate that as much as 25 percent of aerial combat will still be at close range.[37] This puts a premium on agility, even at low speeds at which current high-performance aircraft fly poorly. Low-speed maneuverability technology would make the F-16, for example, a superb aircraft for infighting if advances in Soviet air defenses were to reduce its penetrability. DARPA's X-31 program was designed to provide such technology for the F-16 as well as for the European Fighter Aircraft. The joint U.S.-German program, however, was cut by the Senate Defense Appropriations Subcommittee in the FY 89 budget, and its future remains in doubt.

Concealment

New technology's major contribution to efforts to protect through concealment is low observable or stealth technology. This development is potentially so important that it deserves some detailed attention.

Imagine a combat airplane against which one had to defend but could not detect. One could never be sure: Is it coming? From which direction? Am I a target? Am I ready?

The essence of stealth technology is to escape detection. The more stealth technology can diminish an adversary's capability to detect a target, the less opportunity that adversary has to shoot first. The less opportunity to shoot first, the greater is one's own chance for survival — and victory.

Stealth technology is not, in fact, a single technology. Rather, it is a combination of design, performance, and material characteristics that, when combined, reduce the potential of the system incorporating it to be seen by enemy radar. It is based on advances in a wide range of high technologies — electronics, materials, avionics, and aerodynamic forms — and it is ultimately dependent upon the effective integration of those technologies for success.

The concept of building an aircraft to escape enemy radar detection dates to the mid-1960s when DARPA conducted a number of highly secret studies, which included some flying drones. Airplane designers had already shown awareness of some characteristics that could make a plane less observable, witness the Northrop YB-49 "Flying Wing" of the 1940s. The problem with these older aircraft was keeping them in the air, as their aerodynamic qualities made it impossible to fly them for very long.

A combination of technologies appearing in the 1970s, however, made the concept more feasible. One such technology was the emergence of active control technology (ACT) that allows inherently unstable airplanes to fly. Such equipment is embedded in the F-16. It was further tested in the experimental X-29, whose forward swept wing design demanded that three computers adjust the plane's pitch and roll 40 times per second.[38] If all three computers had failed, the plane would have broken apart in midair.

ACT's introduction allowed designers to overcome the excessive drag and instability that plagued earlier versions of the flying wing. An artist's rendering of the B-2 Advanced Technology Bomber (the Stealth bomber), released by the Pentagon in 1988, suggests that it has exactly this flying wing configuration.

Although keeping an unstable plane in the air is an important requirement for some stealth designs, limiting the plane's visibility is absolutely critical for any design. The key task is to reduce dramatically the plane's Radar Cross Section (RCS). This is not easy, however, because major reductions in RCS yield only limited reductions in the range at which an aircraft can be detected. A 50 percent RCS cut, for example, reduces detection range by only 16 percent, while an RCS reduction of 94 percent is necessary to reduce the detection range by half.[39]

The new designs made possible by ACT contribute to reducing the RCS in that they can create shapes that deflect radar signals away from their source by reflecting radar pulses at oblique angles. A variety of curves or zigzags, therefore, have been introduced into stealth designs, and right angles have been eliminated.

Several other important design features have also been introduced to diminish detection. Engines must be buried in the airframe, for example, with inlets on the top of the wing. Weapons and fuel tanks can no longer be carried externally because they could be seen; they are now carried internally, the weapons in bays. Conventional radar domes and antennae are both electrically transparent and good reflectors, so they have been redesigned by embedding the antennae in the wings and using phased array technology that does not need a moving dish to scan.

Another critical aspect of a stealthy aircraft is the material out of which it is made. Because even the advanced metals used in modern aircraft are relatively susceptible to radar detection, other materials less easily seen have been developed. These include plastic that is transparent to radar as well as radar absorbent composite material based on ferrite or other iron-based materials.[40] These materials enjoy other extremely useful properties in that they are lighter than metal, corrosion resistant, and their directional strength can be tailored to suit particular applications, as in the forward swept-wing. Ultimately, it is hoped that "smart skin," which embeds sensors and systems in the aircraft skin itself, will be incorporated in later generations of stealth aircraft.

Stealth technology's application to air operations is obvious, and if it proves to be successful, air power could be more important than ever before. Although not officially acknowledged, a fleet of 55 to 60 Stealth fighters, the F-19, is already said to be operational.[41]

Advanced Stealth fighter aircraft are expected to fly as early as 1996, and the B-2 Stealth bomber probably will fly sooner. The United States has already selected two teams to produce prototypes of an ATF for the air force, and another competition has been conducted by the navy for an Advanced Tactical Aircraft (ATA). The Europeans also want to introduce stealth technology into their EFA, but it reportedly will take at least eight years for them to develop a variety of state-of-the-art stealth technologies.[42]

One of the major difficulties with stealth development has been its high cost. The Stealth bomber, for example, is now expected to cost $450 million per copy, or 20 percent more than projected.[43] The total ATF program is said to cost more than $64 billion, and some reports have indicated that by the end of the decade, the United States will have invested more than $200 billion in stealth technology.[44]

The high cost of Stealth is said to be one reason that the Congress has been reluctant to procure a second wing of F-19s. Another reason, however, is the belief that technology is moving so rapidly, the current version is already outmoded.

Beyond its application to combat aircraft – whether bombers or fighters – stealth technology might also be applied to autonomous systems, such as reconnaissance platforms, especially drones or remotely piloted vehicles.

The stealthy approach is also being applied to land warfare, where the goal is to reduce the visual, audible, and electronic signature of major systems such as tanks. Despite these efforts, however, tanks will still make a lot of noise. Artist's depictions have also been made available of a stealthy surface ship for the navy. In this instance, too, although some improvements can be made, the prospects for the short-to-medium term are limited.

Protection

A final important way to survive on the battlefield is to ensure that if you are seen and hit, the hit is not disabling.

Recently, a debate has emerged about reactive armor and its implications for the future of tank warfare. Phillip Karber, vice president of the BDM Corporation, has argued, for example, that "reactive armor has rendered obsolete all the [NATO] anti-tank guided missiles in the field today."[45] Others, including the U.S. Army, contend these claims are exaggerated. The new TOW 2 missile with a tandem warhead, they argue, is capable of dealing with the reactive armor problem.

Who is correct in the debate is critical because the investment of billions of dollars will be involved in seeking both to improve tank protection and to overcome it with new generations of antitank weapons. Britain, France, and the FRG, for example, have agreed to go ahead with the TRIGAT antitank guided weapons (ATGW), which is to have a fire-and-forget capability of as much as five miles. How TRIGAT will perform against the reported new Soviet tank with its combination of reactive and composite armor remains an open question. The fact that it took more than a decade to complete a Memorandum of Understanding to proceed with TRIGAT (especially in the face of British reservations) suggests a long way to go before an effective system reaches the field.

The importance of both mobility and protection for survival on the battlefield poses tough choices for force planners. A tank can be protected. The price, however, is a heavy weight that lessens mobility. Whether an optimum balance exists between these two critical characteristics of a tank at a time of the appearance of such capable weapons as MLRS is one of the most challenging questions facing force planners today. In the NATO context, the fact that different countries give greater priority to different characteristics will exacerbate even further the difficulties ahead in the fielding of the next generation of main battle tanks.

Another form of protection, of course, is active defense against attacking weapon systems whether antitank missiles, air defense systems, or antiship missile defense. The combination of more effective sensors, increased accuracy at greater ranges, and a greater variety of potential systems suggests that great promise exists in this area. The unfortunate shooting down of the Iranian airliner over the Persian Gulf, however, dramatically illustrates the limitations that still exist in such advanced systems. The Aegis destroyer is one of the most advanced defensive capabilities available in the world. Yet, it was not able to perform its mission, with tragic results. The incident also demonstrated the sometimes fragile relationship between technologies and the men who use them in combat situations.

Space

The implications for future battlefields of space-related technological developments deserve special mention. Space is already heavily used for communication, navigation, weather forecasting, surveillance, and warning. Developments such as the full deployment of the U.S. Global Positioning System (GPS) are certain to make space-based sensors more powerful, flexible, and available, leading to greater accuracy, speed in communication, and improved mission planning and execution.[46]

Space-based developments will be complicated, however, by the fact that more countries will be capable of utilizing space in the future. The European Space Agency already has registered some impressive accomplishments. France operates the Syracuse 2 military communication system, and Britain, the first country to use a geostationary communications satellite, plans to launch Skynet 4, giving it a capability more resistant to electromagnetic pulse and jamming.[47] Other countries, such as China and India, have also demonstrated their ability to exploit space by launching satellites.

Another development to consider is the use of commercial space assets for military analysis. This has already been done by nongovernment analysts, perhaps the most dramatic example being the study by the Norwegian Institute of International Affairs, which used commercial satellite photography to assess the Soviet military buildup on the Kola peninsula. Commercial satellite photography has also been used by the media to highlight military developments in the Persian Gulf, including the deployment by Iran of Chinese Silkworm missiles.

A major question that must be raised is whether the battlefield of the future will be extended to space. The notion, for example, that space should remain a sanctuary during war has been labeled "romantic."[48] The contributions space systems can make to the performance of terrestrial forces suggest that they will be a target in future conflicts. This, in turn, has led to the emergence of the concept of "space control—the ability to exploit space systems for one's own forces while denying similar support to the enemy"—a concept akin to the traditional notions of sea control and air superiority.[49] Some analysts have argued that the Soviet Union in particular has pursued this capability both through ASAT systems and considerable redundancy in their own capabilities.[50]

According to defense analyst Fred Wisely, reluctance to perceive space systems in a role other than passive support has seriously constrained their battlefield potential.[51] Wisely further contends that, by deploying weapons in space, an adversary would be required to strike targets in yet another dimension if he expected to achieve strategic victory. Considering the uncertainty that must exist about the successful outcome of such a multidimensional attack, deterrence could be reinforced.[52]

The deployment of space-based weapons will be intensely debated for some time. Sentiment is strong for not moving beyond the passive use of space for military purposes. Yet, the leverage that space-based systems might exert on the outcome of the terrestrial battle generates strong pressures for the deployment of at least defensive systems. This debate will remain one of the most fundamental issues facing NATO policymakers as they attempt to shape future battlefields to their advantage.

The Changing Battlefield

New technology is not changing the nature of war, but, in several important ways, it is altering the battlefield on which war will be waged.

Technology is increasing the battlefield's geographic scope. The ranges and accuracies of weapon systems have been significantly enhanced. New sensors have greatly expanded the range of target acquisition. NATO's FOFA concept is explicitly premised on the fact that new technologies now make possible more accurate attack on targets deeper in the enemy's rear areas that previously were not vulnerable.

At the same time, technology is compressing the time for reaction. Furthermore, "technology seems to be leading toward a massing in time rather than space, that is to say, intensity of effort over a discreet segment of space for a finite but heavily used period of time versus many [systems] at the same time at the same place."[53]

The battlefield is also becoming more fluid in that the targets are threatened from more, and sometimes unexpected, directions. This is partially the result of increasing ranges and accuracy. It is also owing to the variety of fire control assets available including unmanned platforms, missiles, artillery, MLRS, aircraft, and helicopters. One trend of the new technology, especially in air combat, is to make "every man a shooter," increasing the scope for individual action.[54]

New technology that is increasing the flexibility and mobility of weapon systems is also increasing the demand for logistical support.[55] The MLRS, for example, is designed to fire a basic rocket with a standard warhead or a scatterable mine, a terminally guided warhead, chemical munitions, and the Tactical Missile System (TACMS). Which will an artillery commander choose? How will he allocate his fire using this system between the close-in battle and the deep battle? How can the logistical system be made flexible enough to deliver the necessary stores where they are most needed?

Moreover, the rate of expenditure of new ammunition is far beyond that of earlier conflicts, thus placing even greater strain on the ability of the logistical system. In NATO's case, the system of the seven nations with forces in central Europe poses a particular coordination challenge because logistics remains a national responsibility. Greater emphasis on maneuver will also complicate delivery munitions to troops who need them most.

Future battlefields will also be more integrated, and combined arms operations will be one of their most salient features. It is already virtually impossible to talk about the land battle in isolation from the air war. Outer space has also become a constant factor, at least for reconnaissance and surveillance. The growing range and accuracy of many weapon systems are also bringing the sea, air, and land battles closer together. Naval commanders, for example, must worry more and more about their defenses against land-based air attack at ranges far greater than before, while they can project power against the shore to an extent never before enjoyed. This more intensive interaction is true not only for surface warfare, but also increasingly for conflicts involving submarines.

The heightened scope, complexity, and integration of future battlefields raise the question of whether such an environment would favor NATO or the Warsaw Pact in the event of a conventional conflict. On one hand, deep or cross-boundary fire capabilities combining lethal submunitions and terminal guidance have potentially an enormous impact that could impede the maneuvering potential of attacking units spearheaded by Warsaw Pact tanks, artillery, and armored personnel carriers. Those indirect fire capabilities, however, could not be expected to blunt a Soviet offensive without some loss of NATO territory, assuming, as one prudently should, that the Warsaw Pact achieved some measure of operational surprise. NATO's doctrine demands that lost territory be regained. This could be done only with an aggressive defense through counterattacks. In counterattacking, however, NATO will expose itself to the same vulnerability through movement that new weapons are designed explicitly to exploit.

It has been said that the history of warfare is the history of the tension between the ability of the attacker to close with the defender and that of the defender to kill the attacker at a distance. The possible emerging situation in which the defender's concentration of fire can be achieved more rapidly than the attacker's (or counterattacker's) ability to close could be producing conditions for a static war of attrition. In those circumstances, especially because inventories of most advanced weapons will be relatively small owing to high costs, the advantage could revert to the side that can bring greater numbers to bear in the shortest period of time. This is not necessarily NATO, which would require several weeks to deliver all of the planned reinforcements from North America and would take even longer to mobilize its greater industrial potential to be decisive.

Conclusion

There is no guarantee that NATO policymakers will correctly decide about technology for the future, either in selecting technologies that will deliver the biggest payoff or in applying them to the battlefield in ways that will exert the greatest leverage. Indeed, the obstacles to managing technology decisions within the alliance successfully are considerable: insufficiently coordinated procurement practices; a mistaken definition of quality that stresses traditional performance characteristics (range, payload, and accuracy) without due attention to sustainability and maintainability; procurement inadequately related at the alliance level to operational doctrine and needs; political difficulties of the kind that emerged with the perception in Europe that FOFA was "offensive"; and economic factors that drive technology decisions unrelated to military need or cost effectiveness. All of these difficulties create a daunting task for policymakers who must make decisions in a world in which change is so rapid that today's most advanced technology is tomorrow's bow and arrow.

That task is made even more complicated by a paradox identified by François Heisbourg:

> [T]he Europeans, essentially the French and the British, have taken major steps toward adopting the new,

more mobile conventional defense resulting from the combination of smart weapons and mobile battlefield C^2. They have not, for their own reasons, made much of the politico-strategic questions of these shifts, treating them rather as natural adaptations to the new state of the art. The Americans, on the other hand, have strongly pushed concepts such as 'Airland Battle' even though the US ground forces remain by and large probably more cumbersome, excessively reliant on firepower, and less adapted to maneuver warfare than some of their European counterparts.[56]

Heisbourg probably gives the Europeans too much credit and the Americans too little. Nevertheless, if the United States and its allies cannot reconcile technology and operations as a coalition, the alliance will face increasing trouble as the technological revolution continues at a breathtaking pace.

The need for an effective technology management strategy in the alliance, therefore, has never been greater. Rising costs, improved performance, and an incredibly dynamic process of change, however, create little room for mistakes.

What is necessary is a clear understanding of how technology fits into the overall picture and its relationship to other critical factors that will bear on the outcome of conflict – such as manpower, morale, and logistics. It also requires an appreciation of what technology can and cannot do. Technology is not a panacea for NATO's conventional problems in central Europe. Moreover, technology will contribute effectively only if the doctrines, structure, and organization are in place to exploit it. NATO's challenge is to create the context so that it can most greatly benefit from the opportunities that the West's enormous technological creativity will provide.

3

Technology Protection and Technology Transfer

THE CASE STUDY: THE TOSHIBA-KONGSBERG AFFAIR

In 1986 the government of the United States learned that high-precision milling machines had been sold to the Soviet Union by the Toshiba Machine Company of Japan. The accompanying computers and software needed to operate the machines had also been provided to the Soviets by Kongsberg Trade of Norway. Together, this equipment provided the Soviet Union with the means to produce high-quality, high-efficiency propellers that allowed Moscow to quiet its newest submarines significantly, dramatically reducing the possibility of detection.

The initiator of the acquisition was Tekmashimport, the Soviet Union's machine importing agency, which sought to acquire advanced milling machines for ship and submarine propellers above existing levels of Soviet manufacturing. In 1980 Tekmashimport contacted Wako Koeki Co., a Japanese exporting company dealing exclusively with Communist countries, to initiate the search for the milling machines. Wako Koeki in turn located the Toshiba and Kongsberg corporations as suppliers of the required equipment.

On April 24, 1981, two contracts were signed in Moscow. The first was between Tekmashimport and C. Itoh and Co. (acting as the agent for the Toshiba Machine Co.), which committed Toshiba to provide four, nine-axes milling machines as well as a five-year service contract.

In return, Toshiba would be paid $17 million—three times the normal price by some estimates.

The second contract provided that for $2 million, Kongsberg Trade, a division of Kongsberg Vaapenfabrik of Norway (a state-owned arms producer), would deliver digital computer equipment to Tekmashimport capable of operating the nine-axes machines. Kongsberg Trade also agreed to provide the propeller design software that would accompany the computers. For arranging the deals, C. Itoh and Co. was paid a finder's fee and then dismissed as the first step in obscuring the illegal transactions.

On May 19, 1983, Toshiba filed falsified license requests with the Japanese Ministry of International Trade and Industry (MITI). Toshiba claimed to be shipping four two-axes milling machines to the Soviet Union for use in civilian industry. Under existing trade laws in Japan and the Coordinating Committee for Multilateral Export Controls (CoCom), the informal regulating organization of Japan and NATO members (minus Iceland) that controls trading by its members with Communist countries, this type of milling machine would have been a legal export (three or more axes machines were prohibited). In fact, each milling head on the machine could be moved through nine independent axes allowing the production of sophisticated propellers up to 30 feet in diameter.

Approximately one year later, Kongsberg Trade applied for permission to export computer control devices for operating two-axes milling machines. The NC-2000 digital computers actually had buried in their microcircuitry the necessary hardware (circuit boards and so forth) for operating the nine-axes Toshiba machines. The propeller design software was written to manufacture propellers using a two-axes machine. This program, however, could be restructured to make full use of the nine-axes equipment, and indeed, in late 1984, Kongsberg supplied the Soviet Union with the improved software.

In 1985 the four milling machines were delivered to the Baltic Shipyards in the Soviet Union. Two of the devices were installed in the civilian sections of the yard by joint Japanese and Soviet engineering teams. At night, however, the Soviet engineers would go to the nearby military shipyards and duplicate on the other two machines what they had done earlier in the day.

For $20 to $25 million, the Soviet Union had gained decades worth of technology, apparently without detection by Western authorities. In December 1985, however, Kazuo Kumagai, a senior executive with Wako Koeki, resigned over a disagreement with his superiors.

Reportedly, it was Kumagai who informed the authorities of the Toshiba-Kongsberg scheme.

As Kumagai's report became public, reactions came swiftly from around the world. National news networks carried stories showing members of the U.S. Congress smashing Toshiba radios on the steps of the Capitol in a graphic display of their displeasure. More substantive reactions within the Capitol soon followed as numerous acts of legislation were introduced specifically intended to punish Toshiba and Kongsberg.

The governments of Japan and Norway also initiated measures to correct some of the damage as well as to deter future illegal technology transfers. Norway closed down Kongsberg Trade's offices and sold all of their nonmilitary business in a corporate restructuring. All software and hardware agreements previously reached with the Soviet Union were terminated. New laws governing technology exports were enacted. The Norwegian prime minister called and apologized to President Ronald Reagan for Kongsberg's role in the affair.

In a move with potentially wide ramifications, Japan agreed to restructure its export control system, a move the United States had been requesting for some time. Tokyo also agreed to increase its financial support of CoCom to a level more commensurate with other members. The Japanese also expressed their intention to increase their documentation to CoCom to levels similar to that of the other members. Japan also announced plans to arrange exchanges of teams of experts to improve Japanese monitoring of other country's exports. They also began to seek criminal prosecution of some of the company executives involved in the affair.

For the punishment of Toshiba, MITI ordered the company to suspend all exports to Communist countries for one year, exports that in 1986 had amounted to 13 percent of Toshiba's total. MITI also ordered that C. Itoh and Co. suspend all machine tool exports to Communist countries for three months. The Toshiba company itself ran full-page advertisements in many of the major U.S. business journals and newspapers apologizing for the affair.

The actions with perhaps the widest ranging repercussions, however, were promoted by the U.S. Congress. On June 16, 1987, Congressman Duncan Hunter (R-Calif.) introduced an amendment to the State Department authorization bill calling for Secretary of State George Shultz to obtain "compensation for damages" from the affair, and the amendment was passed. The lack of strict, punitive sanctions in the House legislation was due, in part, to the intensive lobbying efforts of both the Toshiba Corporation and the Reagan administration. The administration opposed strict penalties because it realized that a demand for compensation would leave the United States open to retaliation and that it would disrupt the voluntary nature of CoCom.

In the Senate, however, Senator Jake Garn (R-Utah) introduced an amendment to the Omnibus Trade Bill that directed the president to impose a government contract ban and an import ban on all goods manufactured by Toshiba and Kongsberg for a period of three to five years. Additionally, these bans were to be applied to any other individual or company that violated CoCom controls between January 1, 1980 and 1987 that resulted in improvements in the East Bloc's submarine capabilities. The amendment allowed exemptions for existing contracts and subcontracts if the president stated that the party involved was the sole supplier of that good, or for reasons of national security. It also authorized the president to seek compensation for damages. The amendment passed 92 to 5.

The damage done to Western security by the Toshiba-Kongsberg affair could not be denied. The Soviet submarine fleet is generally considered inferior to the U.S. fleet, especially because its submarines have been noisy and therefore more easily identifiable and trackable. According to some sources, 90 percent of a submarine's noise level is generated by the propeller. It is precisely because the Toshiba-Kongsberg affair aided the Soviets in reducing this most detectable source of noise that the affair has been called "the most harmful transfer of militarily sensitive technology in over a decade." Combined with the Walker espionage information obtained by the Soviet Union in 1984, the damage to Western security is multiplied many times over.

The Defense Intelligence Agency and Naval Intelligence testified that the Soviets gained 7 to 10 years in propeller development merely from this one transaction. They estimate that the United States will need to spend billions of dollars on antisubmarine warfare over the next 15 to 20 years to counteract the Soviet gains. The need for this increase comes at a time when the Department of Defense budget for 1989 is being reduced by $33 billion. No amount of money can compensate for the diminished lead-time enjoyed by U.S. submarine technologies. As former Secretary of the Navy John Lehman observed: "Their new submarines are virtually as quiet as the subs we were planning to build just a few years ago."

Almost as damaging is the acquisition by the Soviet Union of sophisticated computer boards contained in the Kongsberg controllers.

Although it is not certain exactly what, if any, new computer concepts were given to the Soviets, it seems certain that they have gained another important piece for developing their own sophisticated computers. If the Kongsberg system can be reverse engineered, the Soviets could establish some of the components needed for high-speed computing at levels above what they possess today. Any concepts that might be acquired would, once identified, certainly be distributed throughout Soviet defense industries.

The ease of the Toshiba-Kongsberg transfer raises questions about whether the present Western control system can work. It also highlights the divisiveness that currently exists within the alliance over export controls. These are some of the issues discussed in this chapter.

Introduction

If Western nations are to meet the challenge of effectively bringing high technology to the battlefield on a coalition basis, they must also cope successfully with the dual demands of protecting that technology from potential adversaries and sharing it with one another. Each objective, however, while critical, is made more difficult to achieve by the pursuit of the other.

The case study just presented highlights the enormous difficulties in protecting technologies, yet the critical importance of doing so. The U.S. Department of Defense estimates that although it cost the Soviet Union only between $20 and 25 million to procure the submarine-quieting equipment, it will cost the United States more than $30 billion to upgrade antisubmarine programs enough to track the quieter Soviet submarines efficiently.[1,2]

Although technology protection is considered vital by all members of the Western alliance, the issue has nevertheless generated considerable friction not only between countries but within some nations as well. The running dispute between the U.S. Commerce and Defense Departments, for example, reflects a fundamentally different view of the issue stemming from their different departmental responsibilities.

Within the alliance the friction sometimes takes the form of frustration with failures to protect important technologies as in the Toshiba-Kongsberg case. Friction is also generated by differing allied enforcement policies. Most seriously, however, the United States and its allies have disagreed on the policy level, especially about how restrictive the definition of militarily critical technology should be. At times, as in the case of the Siberian pipeline dispute, these differences can be elevated to the level of major problems. At other times, they represent a low-grade, but persistent, irritant in alliance relations. Whatever their manifestation, differences over technology controls constitute a significant roadblock to the West's attempt to get the most out of its remarkable technological prowess.

Technology protection must be a central element of an overall alliance technology management strategy. As in so many other cases, however, the specific objectives of such protection must be better defined when they clash with other, competing priorities. The issue is not as easy as simply building a fence around everything the Soviet Union might find useful for improving its military capabilities. Political and economic interests also come into play. Striking the proper balance between technology protection and these other interests is one of the formidable tasks confronting Western nations in formulating an effective technology management strategy.

The Soviet Challenge

The Soviet Union recognizes the impact of technology on modern battlefields. The Kremlin is also fully aware of its comparative disadvantage in high technology. Consequently, the Soviets have pursued a multifaceted effort designed to reduce that technology gap. By any measure, the Soviets' investment of resources has been enormous. The result has been to close what had been the Western lead in advanced technology (in computers, for example) of a decade or more to only three to five years in some cases.

In part, the Soviets have based their efforts on improving their own research and development. Future Soviet defense R&D investment is expected to grow at rates exceeding those of the United States.[3]

Another critical aspect of Moscow's effort, however, has been the acquisition of Western technology through both legal and illegal means. According to a 1985 U.S. government study, for example, about 50 percent of more than 30,000 pieces of Western one-of-a-kind military and dual-use hardware and about 20 percent of more than 400,000 technical documents were collected worldwide in response to defined Soviet collection requirements.[4]

The impact of the acquisition of Western technology has helped Moscow in several ways. Not only have the Soviets saved expensive development costs, but they have also avoided in their military industries the consequences of the often sluggish pace of domestic technological innovation.[5,6] The Soviets estimated, for example, that by using documentation on the U.S. F-18 fighter to produce their own look-down/shoot-down radar, their aviation and radar industries saved five years of development and 35 million rubles ($55 million in 1980 dollars), or the equivalent of more than a thousand worker-years of scientific research.[7] In addition, Western technology has enhanced the effectiveness of Soviet weapon systems.[8] That same F-18 documentation (together with F-14 data), for example, provided the impetus to two long-term research projects to design from scratch a new radar-guided air-to-air missile. Finally, Western technology also helps the Soviets develop countermeasures to NATO's own systems.

Once the Soviets cross the difficult hurdle of incorporating new technology into their arsenals, their capability to deploy new systems into the field more rapidly than the West enables them to translate technological advances into battlefield gains with tremendous impact. The outcome was recently described by the U.S. Department of Defense:

> the technological advantages in military capability
> now enjoyed by the West have been threatened, if not
> eroded. . . . The Soviets, although lagging [behind] the
> West in technology, frequently field systems that are
> sufficiently well engineered to meet or exceed the com-
> bat capabilities of Western counterpart systems.[9]

Table 1 presents DOD's estimate of the technological trends
in battlefield systems. Although individual conclusions
might be disputed, the trend is clear. The Soviet closing of
the technological gap with the West, on the battlefield, is
one of the most disturbing trends confronting the alliance.
The West's continuing lead in the laboratory provides little
solace if NATO does nothing to capitalize on its advantage
or protect militarily critical technologies.

The Soviets acquire the bulk of their Western technical
information and technology through legal means.[10] These
legal acquisitions generally have their greatest impact on
the Soviet Union's broad industrial base and thus affect the
military scene on only a relatively long-term basis. Illegal
acquisitions, as in the Toshiba-Kongsberg case, however,
can have a critical short-term impact.[11] Because further
progress in battlefield technology clearly rests in microelectronics and computers, the Soviets have made this a high
priority of their illegal efforts. According to DOD, nearly
half of the Soviet Union's illegal technology trade diversions
relate to computers and electronics, with literally thousands
of pieces of major microelectronics fabrication equipment
obtained during the last 15 years.[12] Most of these illegal
transactions have been facilitated by unscrupulous Western
traders, primarily in Europe but also in Asia as well. Whatever the source, the impact has created a serious problem for
NATO—a reduction in its technological edge on the battlefield upon which it depends critically to offset the Warsaw
Pact's numerical advantage.

TABLE 1
Relative U.S./USSR Technology Level in Deployed Military Systems*

Tactical Systems	U.S. Superior	U.S./USSR Equal	USSR Superior
LAND FORCES			
Surface-to-Air Missiles (SAMs) (Including Naval)		■→	
Tanks		■→	
Artillery		■	
Infantry Combat Vehicles		■	
Antitank Guided Missiles		■→	
Attack Helicopters	■→		
Chemical Warfare			■
Biological Warfare			■
AIR FORCES			
Fighter/Attack and Interceptor Aircraft	■→		
Air-to-Air Missiles	■→		
Air-to-Surface Munitions	■→		
Airlift Aircraft	■→		
NAVAL FORCES			
SSNs	■→		
Torpedoes		■	
Sea-Based Aircraft	■		
Surface Combatants	■→		
Naval Cruise Missiles		■→	
Mines			■

(continued)

71

TABLE 1
(Continued)

Tactical Systems	U.S. Superior	U.S./USSR Equal	USSR Superior
C³I			
Communications		■	
Electronic Counter- measures (ECCM)	■→		
Early Warning	■		
Surveillance and Re- connaissance	■→		
TRAINING SIMULATORS	■		

Source: Adapted from Department of Defense, *Soviet Military Power: An Assessment of the Threat 1988* (April 1988), 149.

*Arrows denote that the relative technology level is changing significantly in the direction indicated.

The Reagan Administration's Response

Upon taking office, the Reagan administration attempted to deal with these trends in two ways. First, it sought to bolster the U.S. military capabilities significantly through a sustained buildup of U.S. forces. Second, it introduced a much more restrictive approach to tighten the flow of technology from West to East.[13]

According to Henry Nau, formerly responsible for international economic issues on the National Security Council staff, the administration's restrictive technology policies were designed to serve three objectives: to protect the new U.S. defense technology investment, to signal U.S. intent to contest Soviet actions that threatened the psychological balance of resolve, and to thwart Soviet foreign policy leverage over the West by preventing excessive reliance on Soviet resources or markets.[14]

Tightening exports of critical technology became a high profile foreign policy objective of the administration. As early as the Ottawa Summit of July 1981, the United States sought to strengthen the export controls administered through CoCom. Reagan administration efforts reached their peak with the creation in 1985 of the Defense Technology Security Administration (DTSA) within the Department of Defense, which defined itself as the focal point of the department's efforts to ensure that international transfers of defense-related technology, goods, services, and munitions were consistent with U.S. foreign policy and national security objectives.

From the very beginning, however, the administration recognized that any success in limiting technology leakage to the East would be achieved only with allied cooperation. Although it initially did not follow up the Ottawa Summit discussion, Washington did seek to coordinate an allied policy toward technology controls during the crisis in Poland. The United States failed, however, and that failure sparked the internal alliance dispute over the proposed Soviet natural gas pipeline to Western Europe. The United States viewed the export of pipeline equipment to the Soviet Union as unnecessarily bolstering Moscow's strength. The Europeans focused not on the strategic implications but on the economic necessity of diversifying hydrocarbon supplies away from the Persian Gulf. Although the issue was finally resolved through a series of studies done at the Organization for Economic Cooperation and Development (OECD), NATO, and the International Energy Agency (IEA), the incident dramatized the different perspectives that have too often characterized the allies' approach to technology transfer.

Competing Western Perspectives

Tension among the allies about technology protection stems from several sources.[15] The primary controversy concerns the definition of "strategic" technology because the

Europeans consider the United States overly restrictive. Technologies that Washington has identified as critical to national security have not been so identified by European capitals. The Europeans argue, as do some in the United States, that defining the list of protected technologies too broadly diminishes the ability to protect effectively what is truly critical. This point was made clearly in 1984 by Norman Tebbit, Britain's minister for trade and industry, when he said, "what we want is greater effectiveness through selecting the things that matter."[16]

An example of the restrictive approach of the United States was provided by a 1987 study of the National Academy of Sciences (NAS). Export controls are supposed to be lifted if it can be proven that the technology in question is readily available outside the United States. As the NAS panel pointed out, however, this rarely happens, for "foreign availability has had virtually no impact on the objective of achieving decontrol." Between 1983 and 1987, for example, 20 areas of technology were thought to be sufficiently global so that they could be decontrolled. The government removed only three from its control list.[17]

The difference concerning definitions is partly a consequence of disagreement about what constitutes a threat. Supporters of less restrictive definitions on both sides of the Atlantic argue that only something with direct military application must be subject to tight control. The U.S. government has contended that anything that even indirectly contributes to the Soviet military capability should be controlled. One European described the U.S. position as the "maximalist conservative security perspective: any high technology is security relevant" in a situation "where communication technologies are integrated into command and control and weapons run with chips are matters of course. . . ."[18]

The definitional problem is only likely to become more acute in the years ahead as more and more technology is appropriate for both military and civilian purposes. That technological innovations are today driven largely by the civilian sector means that dual use technology will become even more prevalent. No one disputes the West's need to protect the latest developments in microelectronics and computers. Yet these are the areas in which disagreement is sharpest because many of the leading innovations are coming from the commercial sector. There is strong pressure to exploit their commercial potential for profit, which was, after all, the reason they were developed in the first place.

This problem of how to manage dual use technology highlights another major source of alliance disagreement about how severely technology transfer should be restricted. Although it is overly generalized to divide the issue into Europe-only or U.S.-only views, the United States – at least the U.S. government – has tended to concentrate on military power, while the Europeans have argued that a healthy Western economic base is a critical factor for ensuring Western security. They contend that technology trade is an increasingly important contribution to a strong economic performance. The issue is the economic cost of technology restrictions.

That there is a cost cannot be disputed. International sales account for as much as 30 to 40 percent of total sales for some high-technology firms.[19] According to Commerce Department estimates, for every $1 billion reduction in U.S. exports, the country loses 25,000 jobs.[20] The NAS report spelled out the logical conclusion for high-technology restrictions. In 1985 controls cost the most dynamic, high-technology sectors of the U.S. economy $9 billion in lost sales and almost 200,000 jobs.[21] This was a conservative estimate of the short-term, direct costs, however, because the overall reduction in GNP as the cuts worked their way through the economy was probably closer to $17 billion. That NAS panel also surveyed 170 companies representing almost one-third of total U.S. technology export sales. It found that 52 percent of the companies lost sales owing to export controls, 26 percent said they had had deals turned down, and 38 percent said customers expressed a preference for non-U.S. sources to avoid those controls.[22] In an attempt to ameliorate this impact, then Secretary of Commerce Malcolm Baldrige consistently called for a 30 to 40 percent reduction in the number of items on the Pentagon's export control list.[23]

Although U.S. companies have been hit hardest, NATO allies are also very sensitive to the economic impact of export controls, especially in light of their concern about the general competitiveness of their advanced technological base. It is not surprising, therefore, that Europeans argue for a broader definition of national, and Western, security, which facilitates a broader definition of what technology can safely be traded without controls.

The direct economic costs of export controls do not suggest the extent of the total damage to the alliance. They do not, for example, consider the negative impact of inefficiencies produced by flows of technology and trade. Nor do they express the intangible costs of strained relations that result between the allies or the opportunity costs of foregone opportunities for alliance cooperation. A climate of uncertainty and suspicion that too often surrounds the issue can have a chilling effect on moves to mount joint projects. François Heisbourg has pointed out, for example, that European concerns over U.S. technology controls "were a factor in inhibiting European participation in the Strategic Defense Initiative and closing the door to U.S. participation in the advanced fighter a European consortium is building for the 1990s."[24]

Organizing for Protection

The cost of export controls has not only been a source of friction between the United States and its allies, but it has also created tension between the U.S. Commerce and Defense departments. These internal U.S. fights have exacerbated the problems allies confront in trying to resolve technology transfer issues with the U.S. government. A critical priority for developing an effective technology protection policy within an overall technology management strategy must be to impose some order in the U.S. government on this issue and to establish clear lines of authority and responsibility.

The United States restricts the flow of critical technology through three major instruments: (1) the Munitions Control List (MCL), administered by the State Department, which forbids the export of weapons and munitions without a license; (2) the Commodity Control List (CCL), which lists sensitive items with obvious military application as well as many dual use items whose military application is less direct; and (3) the Militarily Critical Technologies List (MCTL), which defines technologies of strategic importance that should be subject to scrutiny before transactions occur. The CCL and MCTL are drawn up by the Institute for Defense Analysis, a DOD-based think tank.

The Department of Commerce is responsible for licensing exports of commodities on restricted lists. In the early years of the Reagan administration, however, the DOD began to feel that Commerce Department licensing decisions were too often made with economic interests in mind but little attention to their national security implications. In a positive step, DOD gave the U.S. Customs a $20 million grant in 1982 for Operation Exodus in an effort to improve enforcement of export controls. By 1984, the operation had resulted in 3,182 seizures of high-technology goods illicitly leaving the country having a value of more than $190 million.[25] DOD also began to lobby the White House for a larger role in export license decisions.

On January 17, 1984, Defense Secretary Caspar Weinberger issued DOD Directive 2024.2, which allowed DOD to "treat defense-related technology as a valuable, limited national security resource to be husbanded and invested in the pursuit of national security objectives."[26] The directive was taken as a mandate by Assistant Secretary of Defense for International Security Policy Richard Perle to move DOD more aggressively into trade protection, and the staff of the Technology Security Program under the direction of

Deputy Under Secretary Stephen Bryen was increased from a half dozen to close to 300.[27]

In March 1984 President Reagan granted the Pentagon wider authority to review export license applications for strategic goods. The decision expanded the scope of Pentagon review to include some strategic exports to non-Communist countries. It was made despite opposition from the Commerce Department, which argued that the DOD lacked sensitivity to private-sector business concerns about the detrimental impact of control on U.S. international trade.[28]

The Department of Commerce and the DOD have been at odds about the issue ever since. In 1985, a presidential directive reasserted the primacy of the Commerce and State Departments in the administration of export controls, but the Defense Department kept on fighting. The 1987 NAS report argued that, in fact, "the Department of Defense has overstepped its legitimate statutory role . . . and has exercised de facto veto authority by delaying the review" of export license applications.[29] The findings were disputed by the Department of Defense, and the DTSA continued to assert strong pressures and to criticize Commerce Department decisions about a number of cases. For example, the Commerce Department infuriated the DOD in July 1987 by shifting administration policy on giving Soviet bloc companies the same status as Western firms when it approved 50 licenses for the export of computers and service agreements to the Eastern bloc without clearing them first with the DOD. The Defense Department termed Commerce's action an "egregious lapse of responsibility." In an effort to dampen the interdepartmental warfare, Secretary of Defense Frank Carlucci and Secretary of Commerce William Verity met in February 1988 to review such issues as the two departments' respective roles in licensing, license application processing, defining the scope of technologies deemed subject to control, and related questions.[30]

The DOD also got into a fight with the State Department when the DOD considered an effort to move State's Office of Munitions Control to the DTSA.[31] More recently, the Pentagon attempted to wrest control from the State and Commerce Departments of international sales of commercial jet engine technology, which, the DOD argued, was in many cases identical to that in military fighters.[32]

The internecine disputes in Washington present an administration in disarray to allies that must cooperate with Washington in advancing technology protection. There is neither a sense of who, at any given moment, has the upper hand nor whether technology will be as restricted as the DOD would like to see it or as free flowing as the Commerce Department would propose. At one point, the Commerce Department sought the reactivation of the Export Administration Review Board, created in 1961 by President Kennedy at the cabinet level, to resolve interagency disputes. Some such action is necessary if the United States is to present a coherent policy to allies in CoCom, which itself suffers from some serious institutional difficulties.

Organizing the Allies

There is general agreement that CoCom must be modernized in its procedures and jurisdiction. Some observers argue that the world's technological explosion has made the organization's cumbersome 1950s procedures increasingly irrelevant to modern world trade. Former Under Secretary of Commerce Lionel Olmer, for example, has argued that CoCom is a system that will remain inefficient, particularly as sophisticated technology becomes increasingly available on a global scale, including in areas not subject to CoCom control.[33] One of CoCom's most persistent critics has been West German Foreign Minister Hans-Dietrich Genscher who, for example, told the European Parliament in early 1988 that the organizational controls "go too far."[34]

Progress has been made, however. Spain's decision to participate in CoCom, for example, was an important step, although more industrialized nations—especially the Asian "tigers," Brazil, and India—should be encouraged to join.

The creation of a military group to advise CoCom decision makers on the military implications of various technologies also filled a serious gap in the organization's technical knowledge.

More recently, the Toshiba-Kongsberg revelations prompted movement toward unprecedented consensus on plans to strengthen and streamline controls. On January 27, 1988, CoCom members agreed at a special meeting to reduce the number of items on the list and to do more to protect those technologies that stayed on. This included agreement to tighten technology-export controls, stiffen penalties for violations, share intelligence on suspicious trades, and make stronger efforts to persuade non-CoCom countries to cooperate. According to one estimate, the CoCom changes could ultimately eliminate 36,000 licenses a year for CoCom destinations and another 10,000 for non-aligned but trustworthy countries such as Sweden and Switzerland.[35] At the same time, CoCom members also shortened the list of controlled products by dropping 16-bit microcomputers such as the IBM PC XT and the Apple II GS. The goal, as expressed by one official attending this extraordinary meeting, was "higher fences around fewer goods."

More, however, can still be done to improve the CoCom system. At its core, CoCom's most serious difficulty is enforcement. A major problem is inadequate enforcement assets. At the time of the Toshiba-Kongsberg incident, for example, Norway had only six licensing officials and Japan only ten.[36] CoCom members must bolster these capabilities, perhaps agreeing on a common standard for what is needed to enforce existing rules—especially if they are made more manageable—and how many people would be required. London's *Economist* proposed the sensible idea that it be done on the basis of so many enforcement agents per thousand transactions or so many per $100 million in deals.[37]

Another problem is lack of harmonized enforcement policies. Some countries are much harsher in their treatment of violators of export control than others. The United

States and France are seen as the most vigilant in protecting technology, with Britain not far behind. In a recent case in Paris, for example, four company executives accused of the illegal export of sophisticated machinery that helped the Soviets produce in mass quantity turbine blades for advanced jet engines were charged under a counterespionage law that carries a maximum penalty of 20 years imprisonment.[38] In other countries, the lack of enforcement capability means that a violator faces only a small risk of being caught, and, if he is, he usually faces only a light penalty, perhaps a small fine.

All members of CoCom should institute similar stiff fines for offenders and possible jail terms in egregious cases. The impact of such violations is no less than that of espionage in many cases, and most CoCom countries already have severe penalties on the books for spying. Penalties for export violations should be no less.

More allied coordination of stiffer export control reinforcement is especially crucial as Europe anticipates its greater integration and the elimination of all trade barriers between EC members by 1992, including export licensing. Inconsistent national enforcement policies in such a situation would create too many opportunities for unscrupulous traders to find ways of violating controls without paying too high a price.

If CoCom members are to secure agreement on the need for serious penalties for violation of export control, the violation itself must be seen to be serious. Part of the reason that violations are sometimes winked at is that the technology in question is not considered vital to the Soviet military capability or that it is so available elsewhere that Moscow would have little trouble procuring it. This kind of thinking stems from the undue length of the list of technologies that must be controlled. The fundamental starting point for better allied coordination on export controls, therefore, must be review of the list of controlled technologies. The recent CoCom decision was an important step in the right direction, but the process of paring the list could be carried still further.

The Changing Atmosphere

An important consideration in the degree to which the allies will be successful in enforcing technology controls is the overall East-West atmosphere. It is obviously easier to justify stringent restrictions in periods of coolness or tension in East-West relations than in periods of relative good will.

It is impossible to determine precisely as yet the significance of the improvement in U.S.-Soviet relations manifested in the December Washington Summit and the June Moscow meeting between President Reagan and General Secretary Mikhail Gorbachev. In the short term, these meetings have clearly created an atmosphere in which hopes are high that cooperation between the two superpowers can be furthered. President Reagan's praise of Gorbachev's efforts to advance *perestroika* and *glasnost* establishes a context that suggests more liberal approaches on a number of questions, including overall Western trade with the Soviet Union.

The Moscow Summit intensified a trend already under way. The U.S. Commerce Department, for example, had begun to promote additional opportunities for U.S. business in the Soviet Union. Secretary of Commerce Verity, for example, discussed with Soviet Premier Nikolai Ryzhkov during an April 1988 trip to Moscow a proposal for U.S. construction of oil and gas drilling facilities near Sakhalin Island. At the same time the U.S. government was trying to block a similar project proposed by the Japanese.[39]

A more liberal atmosphere has also been evident in CoCom's approach. The organization, for example, approved a request to license the export of commercial airliners for sale to the Soviet Union. On the heels of that decision, Pratt and Whitney and General Electric requested approval for the release of engine technology that would be incorporated in the new planes—the issue that brought the State Department and the DOD into conflict. A few years ago, these decisions would not even have made the agenda.

Although there is no question that East-West trade can be increased substantially without necessarily adversely affecting NATO security, caution must be exercised. Whether the West should help Gorbachev in his efforts to transform the Soviet economic system into a competitor by the end of the century will be heatedly debated for some time. No one can say for certain whether a fat Russian bear is more or less dangerous than a starving one. Gorbachev is certainly depending on Western technology to help him secure his objectives. Whether alliance nations will cooperate will be determined not only by technology protection considerations but also by continued evidence that Soviet expressions of commitment to a more stable European environment are genuine.

The possibilities for intra-alliance dispute about technology transfer under such circumstances could increase because it will be more likely that economic and security imperatives will collide. Securing advanced Western technology to enhance its military capability remains a high Soviet priority, and there is no justification for opening the floodgates. This is another reason favoring a more streamlined list of controlled technologies, which will eliminate ambiguities that are too often the source of differences among the allies.

CoCom has made important progress as a mechanism for coordinating allied action on export control. The organization is most effective, however, on the technical level. It does not serve as an adequate instrument for making policy. NATO, which has consciously avoided deep involvement on this issue, must become more engaged, despite the wishes of some CoCom members who enjoy the freedom of action that the looser CoCom arrangements allow. The question of technology transfer has become too intertwined with other alliance issues for NATO to continue to keep its distance.

Effective policy on this issue will be developed only if it is related to other critical issues, such as the need to share technology among allies for more efficient development and procurement of armaments. CoCom cannot reconcile these competing imperatives. If an effective alliance management policy is to be developed and implemented, NATO must become more involved. In this respect, a beginning point might be a special NATO meeting to address the close relationship of technology security and alliance defense trade.

4

Arms Cooperation

THE CASE STUDY: THE EUROPEAN FIGHTER AIRCRAFT

On May 16, 1988, Great Britain, the FRG, and Italy signed a Memorandum of Understanding to proceed with the joint development of the EFA, one of the largest all-European armaments cooperation projects ever conceived. The EFA program could represent a giant step forward in NATO arms cooperation as well as in standardizing NATO's defense equipment to meet the challenge of future high-technology warfare. Or, it could be an enormously costly mistake, militarily and financially.

The stakes associated with EFA are high precisely because the project tries to combine several national objectives—economic, military, technological—on a scale not previously attempted in a European cooperative program. How the program came to take its present shape, the problems it has confronted, and the criticisms to which it has been subjected provide a useful case study of the factors at work as the Atlantic Alliance pursues armaments cooperation as a cornerstone of its technology management strategy.

The impetus for the EFA was the recognition by European states that development of a new generation of fighter aircraft would soon have to begin for replacement in the 1990s of their existing inventory of Jaguars, Phantoms, Mirages, and Starfighters. Each European capital, of course, had its own incentives as well: strengthening the nation's advanced technology base, creating jobs, and sustaining a viable aerospace capability. Officials from Britain, West Germany, France, Italy, and Spain met frequently in the early 1980s to search for agreement on military requirements and technical specifications of an aircraft that could be produced in quantities sufficient for economies of scale to reduce its assuredly high price to an affordable level.

Britain, Italy, and the FRG had the cooperative experience of producing the Tornado aircraft, and, although the process was more difficult and expensive than originally anticipated, they were very optimistic that collaboration could be successful. Lurking in the shadows, however, was recognition that none of the countries could afford to develop a competitive aircraft of the next generation on its own and that the alternative to intra-European cooperation was a turn to the United States, something none of them wanted to do.

After a series of meetings begun in late 1983, armaments directors of the UK, the FRG, Italy, Spain, and France had narrowed differing national concepts on the aircraft to the point at which agreement appeared possible. Weight of the aircraft, however, became a major sticking point. All the participants but France wanted a 9.5 to 10 metric ton plane for the European theater. Paris, however, sensitive to the importance to French aerospace of sales outside Europe, preferred an 8.5 metric ton fighter with a more limited engine more suitable for the Third World. The French argued that, with their existing Mirage 2000, another heavy fighter was not needed. The British responded that the type of aircraft the French preferred was too small and underpowered and would not meet the RAF's needs—a view shared by West Germany and Italy.

On July 31, 1985, during a meeting of the five national armaments directors in Turin, France decided to withdraw from the EFA program and go it alone. Underlining budgetary constraints, Paris complained that its air force and navy would get fewer aircraft if they were heavier and more expensive and that such an aircraft would be difficult to sell overseas. Moreover, the fact that the other four nations wanted about 800 total aircraft while France alone wanted 335 entitled France to a larger share of the design, development, and production, a position resisted by the other nations. The French also argued that Avions Marcel Dassault-Bréguet Aviation was the most qualified firm for design leadership among the international teams, a view hotly disputed by the British and Germans.

In December 1985, Dassault unveiled its proposed Rafale-A fighter, an 8.5 metric ton, single-seat, twin engine aircraft. The French aircraft was to be constructed with extensive use of advanced materials such as carbon fiber composites, glass fiber-reinforced plastics, and lightweight metal alloys. By mid-1988, France was prepared to move the Rafale into the preproduction phase, but the company still hoped to attract other European participants and perhaps U.S. industry as well. It offered Belgium, for example, a 10 percent share in the program, although Brussels would not initially be asked to commit itself to acquiring Rafale for its air forces; Brussels was concerned, however, that the price of participation was too high. Paris also was reportedly trying to interest the Norwegians, and France also offered Spain a 13 percent share in the project despite Madrid's involvement in the EFA.

Meanwhile, British Aerospace's Experimental Aircraft Project (EAP) became the developmental forerunner of the EFA. Like the French Rafale, the EPA incorporated many of the latest technological advances in its airframe and avionics. In June 1985 a new company called Eurofighter was formed by British Aerospace, West Germany's Messerschmitt-Boelkow-Blohm (MBB), Aeritalia, and CASA of Spain. Participation in Eurofighter was set at 33 percent each for Britain and West Germany, 21 percent for Italy, and 13 percent for Spain. The shares were based on the number of aircraft ordered, with Britain and Germany each contemplating acquiring 250 aircraft, with 165 for Italy and 100 for Spain, totaling almost 800 fighters.

EFA participants defined demanding requirements for the aircraft. First, it would complement the Tornado in meeting the Soviet threat through the turn of the century. Second, EFA would provide close combat support, have supersonic capability, extended loiter time, air-to-air refueling capability, and a fly-by-wire system to enhance its maneuverability. Third, the EFA would be able to operate away from major air bases, incorporating the ability to land on a road or short runway. Finally, there was the hope—and the intention—of including stealth technology.

At the beginning of the negotiations each participant placed a high priority on different technological aspects of the aircraft: Italy on agility, Germany on supersonic performance, Britain on extended loiter time. By September 18, 1987, however, enough narrowing of differences had occurred to allow the four nations to sign a uniform set of technical requirements for the future fighter. At the same time, air force chiefs confirmed their numerical requirements.

EFA participants hoped to begin full scale development before the end of 1987, but arguments about the plane's engine and radar imposed a delay. Moreover, since the very beginning of the project, doubts had been expressed about the EFA's projected high costs.

Concern about cost was particularly strong in Bonn, especially after the leader of the West German Parliament's powerful budget committee, Rudi Walther, said that an aircraft like the U.S. F-18 could be built under license for far less money. The opposition Social Democrats (SPD) called for scrapping the project. Even in the senior government party of Chancellor Helmut Kohl's Christian Democrats (CDU), warnings were issued that EFA costs had to fall.

In December 1987, Defense Minister Manfred Woerner said Parliament's approval for the EFA could be won, but costs had to be cut. As a consequence, the West German requirement was scaled back to 200 aircraft from the 250 originally planned. This decision reduced the German share of the costs by $2 billion and by more than $500 million in research and development. German defense officials contended that at that level they could fund the program within the limits of their budget without harming other key procurement programs such as the PAH-2 helicopter. Whether or not this is true, however, has been the subject of some skepticism, and it has been argued that Germans might be forced to reduce their planned EFA procurement still further or cut some of their other programs.

Spain also expressed reservations about the cost of the EFA, especially about the level of investment needed to establish the national industrial base necessary to produce the aircraft. The difficulty was particularly acute for Sener, Spain's participant in Eurojet, the EFA engine consortium. As a consequence, Spain did not join the other three participants in signing the protocol to proceed with EFA's full development, making it at least appear open to offers from Paris to participate in the Rafale.

The May 16, 1988, agreement between Britain, Germany, and Italy ended months of lengthy arguments about costs and specifications of the airplane. The approval to proceed was based on agreement to split the work in the proportions earlier outlined. It was also agreed that the fighter would be powered by two Eurojet EJ 200 engines to be manufactured by Rolls Royce, Fiat Aviazione, Motorenund Turbinenunion, and Sener. The forward fuselage would be manufactured by the British, the central fuselage and fin by the Germans, the left wing by the Italians, and the right wing by Spain and Britain. Left unresolved at the time of the signing of the agreement was the decision as to who would develop the fighter's radar, a decision bitterly contested between the Ferranti-led Euroradar group and a team led by Marconi, which proposed a design based on a derivative of the U.S. F-18's radar.

Production was scheduled to begin in 1995. Total cost was estimated by the government participants to be $35 billion, an estimate considered too low by many analysts.

Concerns about the high cost of the EFA prompted the U.S. Defense Department to offer what they considered a cheaper alternative based on a version of the F-18 that came to be called the Hornet 2000. The U.S. argued that the Hornet 2000 could be developed for about one-third the cost of the EFA and half the cost of Rafale.

The Europeans, however, demonstrated little interest in the U.S. option for several reasons. Participation in the U.S. program, they believed, would undermine their capability to maintain a viable aerospace industry. Nor were the Europeans convinced that the U.S. cost estimates were, in fact, accurate; they suggested participation in the U.S. program would be just as expensive as the EFA. The Europeans also arued that the Hornet 2000 would not meet their service requirements. Finally, given past experience, European planners were reluctant to become involved in a U.S. project for fear of the constraints Washington could impose on their overseas sales.

Introduction

"If you want a cacophony, you let each musician choose for himself the key, the tempo, and whether to play fortissimo or pianissimo. If you want operational discord in the armed forces, you build main battle tanks that cannot fire the same shells — as we have done, or different national communications equipment that can't speak to each other — as we have done."[1]

The former NATO Secretary General Lord Carringon's description of NATO's defense procurement scene highlights the fact that defense industrial cooperation has become a necessity rather than a luxury for every member of the alliance, including the United States. Improving armaments cooperation within NATO is a cornerstone of a technology management strategy for the alliance.

From one weapons generation to the next, the cost of the West's increasingly sophisticated arsenal has risen 5 to 6 percent per year. These soaring costs, driven by rapid technological progress, have dramatically reduced the return on the West's collective defense investment. Current

Defense Department estimates, for example, suggest that NATO's current inventory of first-line aircraft will be replaced by the next generation on no better than a 3 : 4 ratio.

NATO'S preferred response to its advancing "structural disarmament" — fewer and fewer weapons at higher and higher costs — has been a revitalization of armaments cooperation.[2] In his first *Report on the Allied Contributions to the Common Defense*, Secretary of Defense Frank Carlucci described NATO's ambitious goals in these defense industrial areas:

> Armaments cooperation programs help to increase efficiency in the allocation and use of Alliance-wide resources, minimize wasteful duplication of effort and promote economies of scale in production. They also improve U.S. and allied defense capabilities and operational effectiveness by access to, use of, and protection of the best technology to meet military requirements with compatible, interoperable, or standardized equipment. Finally, armaments cooperation promotes the military, industrial, and economic viability of allied defense industry upon which we will be dependent in wartime for resupply.[3]

For many years, armaments cooperation was discussed in terms of the "two-way street" between the United States and its European allies, that is, a more equal balance of transatlantic trade in defense items. Recent years have been marked, however, by a shift away from this concept. This is principally owing to unprecedented reductions in the U.S. traditional defense trade surplus with Western Europe: current DOD figures suggest a ratio of current trade on a 1.6 : 1 basis with NATO allies, down from 7 : 1 in the U.S. favor as recently as 1984.

Rather than trade, therefore, today's focus in arms cooperation emphasizes coordination of weapon systems development, from the earliest stages of research through procurement. It is this shift in emphasis that has the broadest implications for NATO's technology management strategy, as Secretary Carlucci noted.

The Foundations of Cooperation

Armaments cooperation is not a new concept in NATO. Indeed, the alliance has recognized the deleterious effect of less than optimal development and procurement of weapons and other defense systems almost since its inception. What is impressive in the last few years is the extent to which NATO has given substance to rhetoric more than two decades old.

The importance attached in Europe to defense industrial cooperation was evidenced in 1972 when members of NATO's Eurogroup agreed to a set of principles aimed at fostering greater collaboration in defense procurement. Among other things, these nations consented to "cooperate in identifying areas where collaboration seems especially important or promising" and to "approach each other when preparing planning requirements to determine whether other members of NATO's Eurogroup have the same or similar intention." Each Eurogroup member also agreed in principle not to formalize its equipment requirements before that country "had satisfied itself that any substantial possibilities of harmonizing have been exploited."[4]

At the time, however, there was more talk than action. By 1974, the unacceptable conditions of alliance defense procurement were dramatized by a report entitled "US/European Economic Cooperation in Civil and Military Technology," which received widespread attention in NATO councils.[5] This report, called the "Callaghan Report" after its author, defense analyst Thomas Callaghan, highlighted the deleterious military impact produced by wasteful duplication of effort in NATO's defense industrial sector. Lack of interoperability, the incapacity of different national forces to communicate with one another, and the limited ability to service one another's equipment were only a few of the highlighted shortcomings. Callaghan recommended a strong move to standardize equipment, and he emphasized the building of a genuine two-way street in arms cooperation. Callaghan's recommendations were echoed in the Culver-Nunn amendments of 1975 and 1976 declaring the statutory policy of the United States to be that U.S. weapons should be standardized, or at least interoperable, with those of the NATO allies and emphasizing the need to make the two-way street concept work better.

In 1975, President Gerald Ford told the third NATO summit in Brussels that, "We must make more efficient, more effective use of our defense resources. We need to achieve our longstanding goals of common procedures on equipment. Our research and development efforts must be more than the sum of individual parts."[6] In that year, the Eurogroup defense ministers also called for a new institution that could become the European terminus of the two-way street, a call that led in February 1976 to the establishment of the Independent European Program Group (IEPG).

The advent of the Carter administration promised renewed efforts at expanding alliance cooperation. Ambassador Robert Komer was appointed NATO adviser to Secretary of Defense Harold Brown. Together with Under Secretary William Perry, Komer gave new emphasis to the subject. At the fourth NATO summit in London in 1977, Carter promised a renewed effort to expand arms cooperation. At the next summit, Carter's new Long-Term Defense Program (LTDP) was approved.

Despite the initial enthusiasm for the LTDP, by 1979 U.S. support for armaments cooperation had hit a new low. In that year the House Armed Services Subcommittee on NATO Standardization, Interoperability and Readiness issued a devastating report on the state of alliance cooperation, which found no redeeming political, economic, or military values in a two-way defense industrial street with Europe. Armaments cooperation was "dead in the water."

It was not until the spring of 1982 that arms cooperation again appeared on the Washington policy agenda. Congress led the way with the passage of the Roth-Glenn-Nunn amendment in the Senate. The amendment called for allied heads of government to agree on a strategy and a structure for improving alliance arms cooperation, as well as policies that ended wasteful duplication and shared more equally the financial and economic burdens of the common defense.

In April 1982 the Reagan administration also turned its attention to NATO armaments cooperation. At that time, a Defense Science Board Task Force on International Industry-to-Industry Armaments Cooperation was established at the Pentagon, chaired by Dr. Malcolm Currie. It was charged with identifying ways for U.S. industry to work more effectively with allied industry in development and procurement of armaments and other defense-related equipment. The task force's report concluded that U.S. technological leadership was deteriorating and that to foster economic and defensive strength, investment had to be increased for long-range research and development. The report also acknowledged a genuine trade-off within a strengthened alliance: increased technological sharing might help establish and inevitably bolster competition for U.S. industry.[7]

About the time this DOD report was completed, David M. Abshire was heading to NATO as the new U.S. ambassador, committed to a revitalization of alliance arms cooperation efforts. Abshire's Center for Strategic and International Studies had a record of promoting armaments cooperation that stretched over a decade. He made improvements in defense industrial cooperation one of his four priorities upon taking the assignment, despite the fact that many old "NATO hands" in Washington and in Europe told him he was foolish to waste his time on an issue that so many people had tried to tackle with such a remarkable lack of success.

Ambassador Abshire has written that the December 1983 meeting of the Defense Planning Committee was a milestone in the efforts to revitalize NATO arms cooperation as part of a broader attempt to improve alliance conventional forces.[8] Of special importance in this regard was the proposal made by West German Defense Minister Manfred Woerner to develop a Conceptual Military Framework to bring order to the plethora of mostly U.S. initiatives with which NATO had recently been confronted, such as Emerging Technologies, AirLand Battle, and Follow-on Forces Attack. Woerner also hoped the CMF would guide NATO planning by looking 20 years ahead rather than the traditional six- to eight-year planning cycle. The CMF would prove important not only for force planning; its impact ultimately would be felt in the armaments planning areas as well.

At about the same time in Washington, Secretary of Defense Weinberger established a core management team—headed by his deputies, first Paul Thayer and then William H. Taft, IV—to oversee the Pentagon's arms cooperation efforts. Thus, the DOD Steering Group for NATO Armaments Cooperation was born. It was the first step in institutionalizing changing DOD attitudes toward the importance of arms cooperation. It also signaled DOD recognition that, even for the United States, arms cooperation was not a luxury but a necessity.

This Pentagon effort coincided with a renewed interest in arms cooperation on Capitol Hill. Senator Sam Nunn had shocked NATO officials with his troop withdrawal amendment in the summer of 1984. This Nunn amendment reflected the senator's frustration with what he saw as a sense of complacency in NATO and an unwillingness to address some serious shortcomings that could lead to military disaster. He made it clear that business as usual would no longer suffice. By mid-1985, however, Nunn was impressed enough by the change in alliance attitudes and the sense of momentum behind conventional defense improvement efforts that he crafted an amendment to encourage further cooperative efforts in the defense industrial arena. The U.S. Mission in Brussels, the Office of the Deputy Secretary of Defense, and the staffs of senators Nunn, Roth, and Warner coordinated closely on the framing of the now familiar amendment to establish a NATO Cooperative Research and Development Program.

The amendment stressed cooperation at both ends of the development process. The bulk of the money – originally $200 million – would be allocated for cooperative projects in the early R&D stages. Another $50 million, however, would also be available for side-by-side testing of competitive U.S. and European systems. This money was "fenced," that is, it would not be made available to the services unless it was spent on research and development programs that involved other NATO allies. The money was to be spent in the United States with the European allies providing matching, although not necessarily equivalent, funds. The intention was to pressure both the U.S. military services and the allies for more defense industrial cooperation.

Senator Nunn, at the time he introduced his amendment, said the Congress would be "watching and waiting" to see the response of the allies and the Department of Defense. DOD was certainly quick to respond. The next year's Defense Guidance, the most important U.S. defense planning document, directed all of the U.S. services to "improve conventional defense by actively seeking cooperative armaments programs with our NATO allies."[9]

The 1985 Nunn-Roth-Warner amendment and the efforts of Senator Dan Quayle to cut through bureaucratic red tape provided a significant breakthrough in alliance cooperative efforts. Since the introduction of the amendment to the 1986 Defense Authorization Act, 12 international Memoranda of Understanding to begin cooperative NATO research and development have been signed. (See table 2.)

Congress has appropriated $445 million for the NATO Codevelopment Programs to date ($200 million more will be authorized for FY 1989), and the Pentagon predicts the U.S. share of current development programs will reach $899.7 million. The allies are expected to contribute $1.77 billion to the codevelopment initiatives.[10]

The NATO Frigate program is potentially the largest NATO cooperative venture in history, with eight nations

TABLE 2
NATO Cooperative Research and Development Projects (as of November 1, 1987)

Research and Development Projects	Participants										
	United States	Canada	United Kingdom	France	Germany	Netherlands	Denmark	Norway	Spain	Italy	Turkey
Ada Project Support Environments	•	•	•	•	•	•	•	•		•	
155mm Autonomous Precision Guided Munition	•	•	•	•	•	•			•	•	•
Modular Standoff Weapons (MSOW)	•	•	•	•	•				•	•	
Multifunctional Information Distribution System	•	•	•	•	•			•	•	•	
NATO Identification System (NIS)	•		•	•	•					•	

96

Standoff Air-
borne Radar
Demonstration
System
(ARDS)

Advanced Short
Takeoff and
Vertical
Landing
Technology

Enhanced
Fighter
Maneuverability

Advanced Sea
Mine

NATO Frigate
Replacement—
1990s

Hawk Mobility
Enhancement

NATO Anti-Air
Warfare
System

Source: Frank Carlucci, *Annual Report to the Congress, Fiscal Year 1989* (Washington, D.C.: GPO, February 1988).

planning to build 50 modern frigates with an estimated total value to the alliance of $20 billion. An additional two dozen projects, including the development of a NATO tactical area communications system and the upgrade of the F-16 fighter aircraft, are in various stages of negotiations to become cooperative programs. In total, the Pentagon has planned to dedicate nearly $3 billion through 1992 for this type of NATO cooperation.[11]

The real importance of these so-called Nunn programs is not just that they are cooperative efforts, but that they are linked to NATO's agreed critical deficiencies. These deficiencies were agreed by NATO officials as part of their 1985 Conventional Defense Improvements effort.[12] Each cooperative program—whether it be the autonomous precision-guided munition, the system to identify friendly and hostile aircraft, or the NATO Frigate program of the 1990s—targets an identified alliance military need.

Not all of the Nunn amendment programs, however, have been an unqualified success. West Germany, for example, is threatening to withdraw from the Modular Standoff Weapons (MSOW) program, a move that NATO officials argue would cause the air-to-surface missile project to collapse. A German withdrawal, they contend, would neutralize partner nations (the United States, United Kingdom, and Italy), unable to absorb the 22 percent share of the project currently assumed by Bonn. Apparently, Bonn is under heavy pressure from Paris to join with France in the Apache-container weapon system—a short-range missile, submunition-ejecting system—comparable to the MSOW's short-range version.[13] France pulled out of the MSOW program in 1988, and Canada shortly afterward.

A major challenge to the alliance remains to bring the Nunn programs to fruition. A worrisome development in this regard was the cancellation by the Senate Defense Appropriations Subcommittee of the U.S.-German X-31 program in the FY 89 budget. The X-31 program was intended to be a demonstrator of new technology for enhanced fighter maneuverability at slower speeds. A prototype was to fly in 1989. Before becoming a cooperative program, the FRG's MBB spent more than $40 million on the technology. The action of the Senate Subcommittee so bothered the Germans that German Defense State Secretary Manfred Timmermann wrote to U.S. Deputy Secretary of Defense Taft — the two officials responsible for armaments cooperation in their respective countries — saying that he had "deep concern" and that it would be "highly disturbing in times of decreasing defense budgets that transatlantic cooperation would suffer setbacks." He expressed his hope that the X-31 program would be reinstated, making it the first Nunn amendment program to come to fruition.

Despite these problems, the Nunn-Roth-Warner amendment represented a major step forward in arms cooperation. It energized the process at a critical moment, and it demonstrated the alliance could put its money where its rhetoric was.

Another promising development is the establishment of the Conventional Armaments Planning System (CAPS) at NATO Headquarters. NATO's force planning process has made great strides in this decade; the CMF increased the alliance planning horizon from 6 to 20 years, and the Conventional Defense Improvement effort allowed NATO to evaluate how well individual allies were doing to overcome the mutually agreed critical deficiencies. Together, these innovations provided alliance policymakers with important tools to identify and attack NATO's most serious military shortcomings. The next step, as Lord Carrington correctly suggested, was to link NATO force goals more effectively with national armaments planning.

In mid-1987, Lord Carrington proposed the creation of an alliance armaments planning system, arguing that a closer link between force planning and armaments decisions would "create optimal opportunities for enhanced cooperation."[14] Although some allies had reservations about parts of the secretary general's proposal, at the December 1987 meetings of the Defense Planning Committee and North Atlantic Council, alliance defense and foreign ministers approved a two-year trial period for a Conventional Armaments Planning System.

Under the chairmanship of Assistant Secretary General for Defense Support Mack Mattingly, a Conventional Armaments Review Committee (NCARC) will oversee a process that will analyze new national armaments goals and propose a NATO Conventional Armaments Plan (CAP). The purpose of the plan will be to identify specific opportunities for cooperative endeavors after a comparison of national armaments planning. It will also highlight areas in which NATO force goals are not being translated into national armaments goals.

Under the new system, NATO nations will identify their need for an operational capability that might be met by the development, upgrade, modification, or other acquisition of military equipment. A reply to an Armaments Planning Questionnaire (APQ) – similar to the Defense Planning Questionnaire on national force plans that has been a NATO planning tool for years – will then be submitted to describe national plans and programs to meet established armaments goals. The Review Committee oversees the analysis of the national submissions and the drafting of the CAP. In this manner, NATO is moving toward the linkage of force planning and armaments planning described in figure 3.

The Impact of Improved Armaments Cooperation

Armaments cooperation within NATO is profoundly affecting the way allied governments and industry do business, forging the beginnings of an alliance defense industrial base. During the last five years, for example, 15 percent of the military equipment procured annually by the British Ministry of Defense has been collaboratively produced with the allies. Another 10 percent of British military equipment is purchased directly from overseas industry.[15]

On the U.S. side, despite the declining U.S. defense trade surplus, the Pentagon's program of side-by-side test-

FIGURE 3
Force Planning and Armaments Planning Interaction

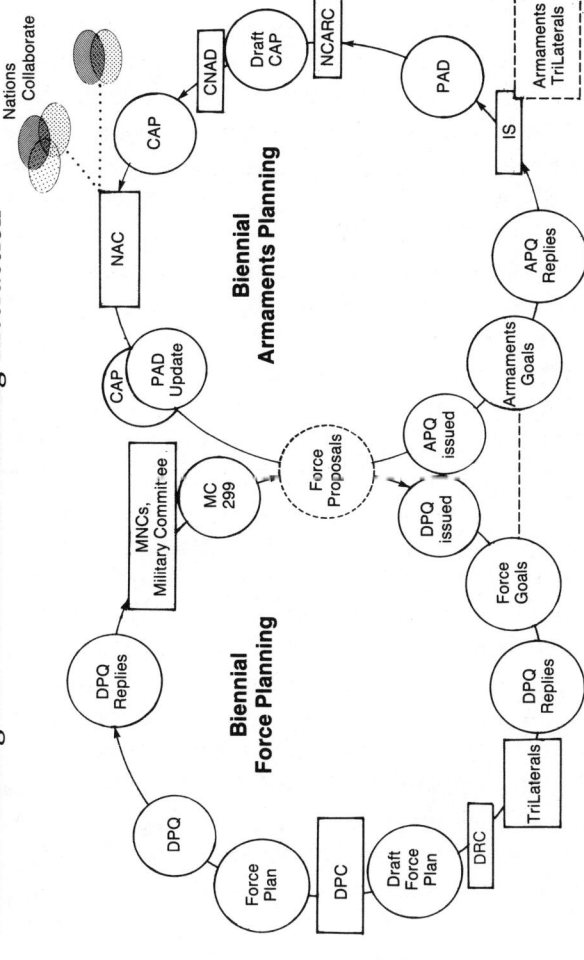

Source: U.S. Department of Defense, 1983.

APQ – Armaments Planning Questionnaire; CAP – Conventional Armaments Plan; CNAD – Council of National Armaments Directors; DPC – Defense Planning Committee; DPQ – Defense Planning Questionnaire; DRC – Defense Review Committee; IS – International Staff; MC 299 – Military Committee Document; MNCs – Major NATO Commanders; NAC – North Atlantic Council; NCARC – NATO Conventional Armaments Review Committee; PAD – Planning Analysis Document.

ing of existing U.S. and European equipment is expanding rapidly. There are currently 49 allied systems under evaluation in Pentagon test programs, and the Defense Department estimates that they will be evaluating 70 allied systems during the next fiscal year. The latest Pentagon Selected Acquisition Report (SAR) on major weapons purchases reflects the increasing returns on joint industrial effort. Some $33 billion was planned for five transatlantic purchases: the AV-8B Harrier (McDonnell Douglas, British Aerospace, and Rolls Royce), the Army Mobile Subscriber Equipment (GTE and Thomson-CSF), the T-5 trainer aircraft (McDonnell Douglas and BAe), the KC-135R re-engining program (Boeing and CFM International), and the Martin Marietta/Oerlikon system, which appears to have won the army's forward-area air defense competition.[16]

Much of the progress in Washington can be traced directly to the efforts of Deputy Secretary of Defense Taft. Chairing both the DOD Steering Group on NATO Armaments Cooperation and the Defense Resources Board, the deputy secretary was able to press the alliance cooperative agenda with the occasionally resistant military services.

Taft's appearance at a 1985 "reinforced" North Atlantic Council meeting that was devoted specifically to armaments cooperation marked the first time since 1950 that alliance deputy defense ministers had met under such terms. Most important, it was not a one-time event, but developed into a series of meetings that ensured that progress could be reviewed and outstanding issues addressed by political decision makers above the level of technical experts. Armaments cooperation was thus elevated to a priority position on the alliance agenda. This development was reinforced when the IEPG also met at ministerial level, something many analysts had never expected to happen.

The resurgence of interest in arms cooperation in the mid-1980s was clearly the product of several factors: the need to find a cost effective response to the continued growth of the Warsaw Pact conventional threat, increasing constraints on national defense budgets, the shift in

NATO's attention from theater nuclear modernization to the conventional component of deterrence, and the desire to improve national technological capabilities.

The Future of Alliance Armaments Cooperation

Despite the historical commitment of NATO member states and impressive recent progress, transatlantic armaments cooperation efforts are at a watershed; U.S. programs to engage the allies in codevelopment projects and alliance attempts to institutionalize joint planning are facing growing challenges from commitments to intra-European cooperation, attempts on both sides of the Atlantic to protect the domestic industrial base, and pressure on the flow of advanced technologies.

One difficulty that continues to plague NATO in this latter regard has been the inability to harmonize technology sharing and technology protection on an institutional basis. Loud complaints can still be heard that restrictive technology transfer constraints, especially in the United States, have impeded efforts to enhance defense industrial collaboration. Decisions are made on an ad hoc basis, and there is no real system that has established criteria for determining when advanced technology may or may not be shared in a cooperative program.

An important step was taken to overcome this problem in the case of the radar system for the Rafale and EFA. In May 1988, Secretary of Defense Carlucci sent a letter to his British, West German, Italian, and Spanish counterparts indicating that because they were participants in the EFA program, the United States was prepared in principle to supply them with the technology necessary to produce an advanced version of the Hughes AN/APG-65 radar. The decision to release the technology was the result of a new practice established at DOD for reviewing technology transfer cases. That practice involved the creation of a matrix to rank the consequences of losing specific radar technology elements, including manufacturing technology, to the Soviet bloc and to estimate how these consequences would become less serious over periods of 5, 10, and 15 years.[17] Many people in the Pentagon hope that the decision on the APG-65 will serve as an important precedent for future decisions to release and share important technologies.

Vastly improved technology security arrangements will be necessary if transatlantic armaments cooperation is to transcend the current level of technology sharing. As a beginning, a major NATO conference, bringing together national governments and industry – with ministerial participation – is needed to address the broad agenda of technology protection policy and the structure of alliance defense trade.

Another major concern to many who propose greatly expanded cooperation among the allies is the number of secret or "black" research programs being conducted by the United States. Some defense analysts have suggested that black programs, funded at perhaps $19 billion in 1987, represent 25 percent of the current U.S. defense R&D budget and are projected to grow by 4.3 percent through 1989. Already, for example, the U.S. air force has more than a third of its research budget in classified programs.[18] The danger is growing, therefore, that alliance efforts to merge new research and development programs through cooperative programs could be derailed at some future date when the U.S. Army, Navy or Air Force reveals the result of its own parallel, secret technology development program.

A profound handicap in forging any new alliance arms cooperation initiative at the research and development stage is the continuing drain on scarce defense R&D resources produced by duplicative national efforts in Europe. As the 1987 report of the IEPG, "Toward a Stronger Europe," suggested, the lack of a common or coordinated European research program is one reason that NATO Europe is able to afford collectively only one-third as much military R&D as the United States, though the intra-European arms market is roughly 40 percent of U.S. procurement.[19] Indeed, the report argued that it seems "that a nation will support the interests of Europe as a whole only when it is in their national interests to do so" and that support of existing employment levels and the preservation of technological capabilities are major motivations for sustaining uneconomical national production capabilities. A recent study of the U.S. NAS confirms this assessment, suggesting that duplication of effort by the European defense industry costs $36 billion per year, or roughly just under one-third of NATO Europe's defense spending.

Declining or stagnant defense budgets throughout the alliance lend an urgency to finding a solution to this problem. In confronting it, however, the Europeans face a dilemma. European policymakers seek to attain the two goals of safeguarding Europe's technological competence while acquiring effective arms at the best possible price. In many cases, however, one goal can be achieved only at the expense of the other. Therefore, the Europeans face a choice of selecting cheaper options, generally weapons systems programs purchased directly from, or developed in cooperation with, the United States, or cooperating with one another and safeguarding Europe's defense industrial base, realizing that the costs are likely to be higher—considerably higher, in some cases.

There are, of course, inherent tensions between a European approach and efforts to expand transatlantic cooperation. European allies, especially those with larger populations, scientific establishments, and gross national products, are under increasing pressure to protect their national industrial bases as the worldwide market for sophisticated arms becomes more competitive. Increasingly, intra-European cooperation and the creation of an integrated European arms market are seen as the way out of this industrial dilemma. As the IEPG report argued, reflecting what is probably a broad and growing consensus in Europe, a vigorous program to expand intra-European arms cooperation is the first, necessary step toward a strong and independent "European Pil-

lar" (within NATO), which could become an effective partner of the United States.

Europeans argue that intra-European cooperation is
both natural and necessary. As that cooperation bears fruit,
however, the United States might find itself outside some
important projects. The Europeans argue this is not meant
to be anti-American, but that it is essential if Europe is to
get its act together. In an atmosphere soured by persistent
trade deficits and perceived European protectionism, such
measures might spark a U.S. reaction. A cycle could be
created that produces increasing discord among allies in an
area that should be the hallmark of harmony.

Approximately 20 all-European collaborative research
and development programs are now sponsored by the
IEPG. Among the most advanced of the European development programs are a Franco-German antitank helicopter
(total program cost: $5.4 billion), the British, French, and
German effort to develop the next generation medium-
range antiarmor missile, and a quadripartite program to
build a transport helicopter for the 1990s. In Munich, a
Joint Armaments Agency has been established to manage
three intra-European cooperative ventures including the
Franco-German helicopter program.

In addition to the IEPG efforts, bilateral cooperation
among the Europeans has also increased. Britain and
France, for example, which between them account for more
than 80 percent of defense R&D in NATO Europe, held an
unprecedented series of meetings starting in the autumn of
1987 focusing on reciprocal procurement.[20] Interest in reciprocal procurement—between two countries that bought virtually nothing from each other—is driven by the desire to
avoid duplicative development on one hand and to promote
competition on the other. The two countries are also cooperating on major projects (often with other allies) such as the
Cobra counterbattery radar, and they are encouraging companies to get together as British Aerospace and Thomson-
Bréguet seem to have done for developing 120-mm mortar
ammunition.[21] Discreet talks have also occurred among

Britain, France, and the United States about a new air-launched nuclear missile.

While intra-European cooperative programs have multiplied rapidly in the mid-1980s, the process of building the European pillar in NATO confronts substantial political barriers. Disagreement about operational requirements for military equipment, lack of information about national equipment replacement and modernization schedules, and fragmented research and development efforts are only some of the barriers to a more integrated European arms market cited by the IEPG report.[22]

One of the most important, and almost axiomatically the most controversial, intra-European codevelopment programs underway is the EFA effort. The EFA program symbolizes all of the tensions between intra-European and transatlantic cooperation. At perhaps more than twice the cost of upgrading the performance of the U.S. F-18 fighter, the EFA appears to the Pentagon to be a long-term wasteful drain on scarce European resources for conventional force improvements. It considers the "opportunity cost" of the EFA enormous in light of all of the other conventional force improvements that are necessary but for which there will be, as a result of EFA, little money. The European allies counter that U.S. offers of collaboration on upgrading the F-18 are no more than an attempt to destroy forever any allied capability to produce top-of-the-line fighter aircraft.[23]

A key issue in the debate over the EFA, but also in the larger context of the challenges of intra-European versus transatlantic cooperation, is the degree to which today's major collaborative weapons development programs are becoming what Dennis Kloske, U.S. deputy under secretary of defense (planning and resources) has termed "industrial entitlements." Kloske's concern is that these major weapons programs are increasingly being designed to secure jobs or an advanced technology base, rather than as economically efficient responses to critical NATO military requirements. For example, the West German defense minister's final recommendation to the cabinet on participation in EFA cited the program's critical role in fostering future German and European defense aerospace industry competitiveness; it made no mention of how it would meet military requirements. In announcing the EFA go-ahead in May, German Defense Minister Woerner reinforced the notion when he said that the EFA project was a major contribution to the "sustainability and survivability" of Europe's aerospace industry and that protecting that industry was "a very critical facet of maintaining Europe's position in world affairs."[24] West German planning already reflects the trade-offs involved in the EFA purchase. According to press reports, approximately 100 other equipment programs – including the next generation main battle tank – will be either cancelled or postponed to pay for the Federal Republic's 200 EFA aircraft.[25]

Another element of the tension among the NATO allies on issues of intra-European armaments cooperation is the possibility that the creation of a single European market, scheduled for 1992, will challenge the still fragile NATO framework for cooperation across the Atlantic. Recent moves by the European Economic Community appear as possible harbingers of an effort to include defense industry in a single market protected from North American competition. The European Commission's consideration of a measure that would in effect require additional customs duties for imported U.S. defense equipment is feared to be only the first step in this direction.[26]

Mr. Karl-Heinz Narjes, the outgoing EC commissioner for industry, made little secret of his interest in expanding the Community's purview to include defense industry through the EC's ongoing industrial and information technology programs.[27] Narjes has said that it is "unthinkable that military R&D and the production of weaponry should not be part of the whole process" of the 1992 internal market development. "We cannot deprive our defense industry," Narjes concludes, "of the benefits we seek for our civil industries."[28] One of the key ways the EC will attempt to bear on defense cooperation is through the planned liberalization of public procurement in which defense procurement accounts for a substantial portion.

The fact that many of Europe's leading companies preparing for the 1992 target are major players in both civilian and defense business will make it impossible to keep defense unaffected by the drive toward a single market. If Daimler Benz acquires MBB, for example, which the Bonn government is encouraging it to do, it will not only be interested in selling its Mercedes throughout Europe, but it will also become West Germany's largest defense company with a turnaround of around DM 75 billion.[29]

This dual nature of Europe's leading industrial firms will be felt especially in the electronics sector. A rationalization of Europe's electronics industry will make it a more competitive producer of key components. In January 1988, for example, Matra, the French defense electronics group, was privatized and sold small stakes to a "core group" of shareholders including Britain's General Electric Company (GEC), Daimler Benz, and the Wallenberg Group of Sweden. All of the companies that bought into the deal say they saw their stake in Matra increasing both their competitive capabilities and defense cooperation.[30] U.S. defense industry has also begun to recognize that 1992 will change the shape of transatlantic trade by strengthening European industry's ability to compete.[31]

A strategy to expand alliance armaments cooperation must establish an environment conducive to industry-to-industry initiatives. Defense industry remains far ahead of national governments in forging efficient international consortia. Consequently, reducing impediments to even greater international industrial cooperation and increasing industry input in government-to-government cooperative negotiations should be priorities for NATO defense planners. A crucial first step to unleashing private industry cooperative initiative is a thorough review and reform of U.S. government technology export licensing procedures.

Other industry observations and complaints about the current structure of alliance armaments cooperation efforts must also be addressed. Critics of current arms cooperation point to the French withdrawal from the group of nations comminted to producing a NATO MSOW and the possible U.S. Air Force exit from the cooperative program on part of NATO's Identification System (NIS) as evidence that existing transatlantic cooperation is poorly constructed, attempting to merge too many disparate national requirements. Skepticism about the actual economic efficiency of many NATO programs is another byproduct of industry experience with current codevelopment efforts.

In short, NATO governments must create the institutional framework for a more effective government-defense-industrial consultation on arms cooperation issues. As the European allies move toward the inevitable merging of defense acquisition and the creation of a common armaments market, a forum is needed to provide input into the process for the defense industry—European and American. The NATO Industrial Advisory Group exists in Brussels and could be the focus of an alliance effort to upgrade the defense industry role in NATO armaments cooperation planning. In a similar vein in *Toward a Stronger Europe*, the distinguished IEPG study team suggested that an advisory group of European industry representatives would be helpful in steering the course of intra-European cooperation.[32]

5

Conclusion

Reflecting on Germany's success against a France that was at least its equal technologically in the early days of World War II, Winston Churchill observed: "I did not comprehend the violence of the revolution effected since the last war by the intrusion of fast moving armor. I knew about it, but it had not altered my inward convictions as it should have." Churchill's comment draws attention to one of the most fundamental features of warfare. Victory on the battlefield does not go to the technologically superior, but to those combatants who have taken what is at hand—the weapons, the doctrine, the men, and the organizations—and molded these effectively into a single entity. It is the bringing together of many innovative ideas, merging these ideas with the opportunities offered by technological advance—often already reflected in equipment—molding organizations, training men, and ultimately creating a combined arms capability that ensures success.

On a battlefield populated by allies as well as adversaries, success will depend on how those allies have worked together to integrate these factors. Technology development alone, even across the enormous spectrum now being pursued by NATO members, will not be enough. The key to the success of NATO's technology management strategy will be how well the allies—as a coalition—integrate technology into the larger mosaic of manpower, logistics, doctrine, operations, and tactics.

NATO does not have to begin from scratch. Two programs in particular that are quite promising as progressive efforts to meld new and emerging technologies with tactics and operations are the Balanced Technology Initiative and the Competitive Strategies program.

The Balanced Technology Initiative

The Pentagon's Balanced Technology Initiative (BTI) is the current vehicle for strengthening and focusing advanced U.S. technology research in conventional weapon systems and military equipment. An initiative of the Senate Armed Services Committee, BTI had its origins in the 1986 debate about the proportion of the military R&D budget devoted to strategic defense. Members of Congress were frustrated that more had not been done to explore the implications for the conventional battlefield of the research in advance technologies conducted under the Strategic Defense Initiative. In mandating a shift of resources toward basic research on conventional weapons and equipment, Senator Nunn's committee argued:

> if NATO is to find ways to reduce its current reliance on the threat of early use of nuclear weapons, it must harness its collective technological capabilities to counter quantitative advantages that provide the Soviet Union and its Warsaw Pact allies with a destabilizing capability for a short-warning conventional attack. The Balanced Technology Initiative is designed as a high priority response to this threat.[1]

Congress allocated $200 million in the 1987 defense budget for BTI; to begin the program, the Pentagon selected 48 projects from 250 candidates offered by the Office of the Secretary of Defense, the Defense agencies, and military services. In 1988 Congress also appropriated $100 million to continue original BTI research programs and identify possible new starts. Prospects are good that the Pentagon's 1989 request for $238 million will emerge from the congressional budget conference unscathed.

The Pentagon was initially skeptical of this new congressional initiative and unwilling to reorganize R&D efforts radically on the basis of a last-minute adjustment to the 1987 defense budget. It has come to recognize, however, the potential of the BTI framework for defense R&D efforts, which enjoys obvious support on Capitol Hill. In the president's 1989 budget request, BTI was identified for the first time as a line item in the Pentagon budget. Institutionally, the Office of the Under Secretary of Defense for Research and Advanced Technology has made remarkable progress in disciplining the selection of the most promising projects in terms of the criteria of the 1987 legislation, which included a strong focus on "smart" munitions and antiarmor technologies.

BTI research efforts are organized into five broad technology areas:

- smart weapons;
- armor/antiarmor;
- reconnaissance, surveillance, and target acquisition/ battle management, communications, command and control (RSTA/BMC³);
- high power microwaves (HPM), designed to help understand the effects of HPM on weapon systems and place vulnerable enemy systems at risk; and
- special technology opportunities, a category capturing projects that might have important conventional impact such as advanced cruise missiles or high energy lasers.[2]

One of the key objectives of the BTI program is to support promising new technologies that can have a positive impact on NATO's most urgent requirements. In this regard, the BTI has linked its areas of technology research to the nine key mission components outlined in SACEUR's Conceptual Military Framework. These mission components include military contributions to crisis management, defeat of the lead echelon, attaining and maintaining a favorable air situation, FOFA, sea control, maritime power projection, control and protection of allied shipping, flexible response beyond conventional defense, and rear area operations. The matrix constructed to identify the relationship of BTI's five program areas and the nine mission components shows that each of the BTI projects can contribute to at least three, and often more, of SACEUR's nine major requirements.

Competitive Strategies

Complementing the BTI as part of U.S. strategy to link advanced technology to operational concepts is the Competitive Strategies study. The basic objective of this study is to match the strengths of U.S. and allied technologies and operational concepts against enduring Soviet-Warsaw Pact battlefield vulnerabilities.

Competitive Strategies is based on assumptions of a long-term competition with the Soviet Union of which the military dimension is only one component and there are only limited resources on both sides. It focuses on important changes in policy, doctrine, and technology to produce both a peacetime and a wartime impact on the actions of the Soviet Union. In peacetime, the program seeks to identify ways to force the Kremlin's military investment into areas of comparative disadvantage and to reduce Moscow's flexibility to redirect defense resources rapidly to counter new developments by NATO. In wartime, the goal would be to provide the means to disrupt the sequence of Soviet offensive operations, giving NATO the time it needs to mount a robust defense.

The study's initial Task Force on Mid-to-High Intensity Conflict in Europe sought to identify the priority tasks of

Soviet forces arrayed against NATO, find the vulnerabilities of those forces, and define possible points of NATO leverage. Its goal was not to take a static snapshot of the situation, however, but to assess how the process would develop over time. Therefore, the task force sought not only to formulate possible U.S. initiatives, but to predict Soviet responses in doctrine, tactics, deployment, and acquisition and then to identify U.S. counterresponses.

The task force report, still classified, identified three priority areas for the application of new NATO technologies: countering the Soviet air offensive; blunting enemy penetrations of NATO's forward defense; and disrupting East Bloc troop control and operations.

The implications of these priorities for technology development programs are already clear. Countering the Soviet air offensive means countering Soviet force concentrations and disrupting the tempo of operations at their main operating bases. This can be done through greater emphasis on standoff weapons and unmanned remotely piloted vehicles. Blunting Soviet penetrations on the ground can be achieved by making covering forces more agile and more lethal. This could be accomplished through some combination of longer-range mass fire systems and better minelaying capabilities (making the process instantaneous). Antiradar attack systems and new penetrating warheads for NATO weapons will prove especially effective against Warsaw Pact strategic (theater) command, control, and communications facilities, making their troop control much more difficult.

The recommendations of the Competitive Strategies' first task force report have been reviewed by the Office of the Secretary of Defense, the military services, and the operational commanders. A war gaming committee is now preparing recommendations on an operational concept to employ new technologies that could be fielded by the late 1990s. The development of this operational model will be the basis for a follow-on costing exercise and eventual impact on the development of the budget.

Although the second phase of the Competitive Strategies study will look at future non-nuclear strategic systems, the impact of this first phase of work on the future European battlefield is extremely important to the NATO allies. For the first time, the Pentagon has a framework for translating emerging technologies into force multipliers in support of NATO doctrine.

If the Competitive Strategies effort and BTI are to have a major impact on alliance conventional defense capabilities, they must be placed within a NATO framework that engages the United States' European partners. For its part, the United States must review the range of its advanced R&D projects and identify specific BTI technologies that could be most easily exploited in cooperation with the allies. Some new technologies will remain too sensitive to share even with NATO allies, but the United States must identify areas for a freer flow of information and technology among NATO partners.

BTI can drive an exciting new effort in NATO arms cooperation if alliance leadership is forthcoming. The idea of expanding the BTI program to include a NATO cooperative focus was first raised in a September 1987 study by the Center for Strategic and International Studies that recommended to the Pentagon and Congress that a portion of BTI funding be earmarked for new collaborative programs.[3] Appearing before the Senate Armed Services Committee on October 7, 1987, Deputy Secretary of Defense Taft stated that the DOD would have no difficulty with such an approach. This was confirmed in Secretary Carlucci's 1988 "burden-sharing report" to the Congress when he wrote,

> The Balanced Technology Initiative is another new defense program that is addressing many problems of considerable importance to our NATO allies. This program was explicitly established to support the development of technologies important to conventional defense. . . . In continuing the BTI program, we plan to establish cooperative technology development efforts with our NATO allies.[4]

In fact, the creation of cooperative programs under BTI will be absolutely necessary if the Pentagon is to achieve its recently stated goal of having 25 percent of its research, development, testing, and evaluation budget devoted to international programs by 1999. The rapid expansion of cooperative R&D projected in the Pentagon, shown in figure 4, from today's 4 percent to 10 percent of the total budget by 1994, will depend especially on success in coordinating advanced technology development efforts. As the electronics-related components of U.S. military research in particular rise to nearly half of the Pentagon's RDT&E budget by the late 1990s, BTI programs to develop software-intensive battle management and intelligence gathering systems should form the basis for expanding alliance cooperation.[5]

Unfortunately, NATO as an institution has not been in a position to act quickly on the proposal to move armaments cooperation to areas of more advanced technology. The sys-

FIGURE 4
Cooperative Research and Development
(Percentage of Research, Development, Testing, and Evaluation [RDT & E] Budget)

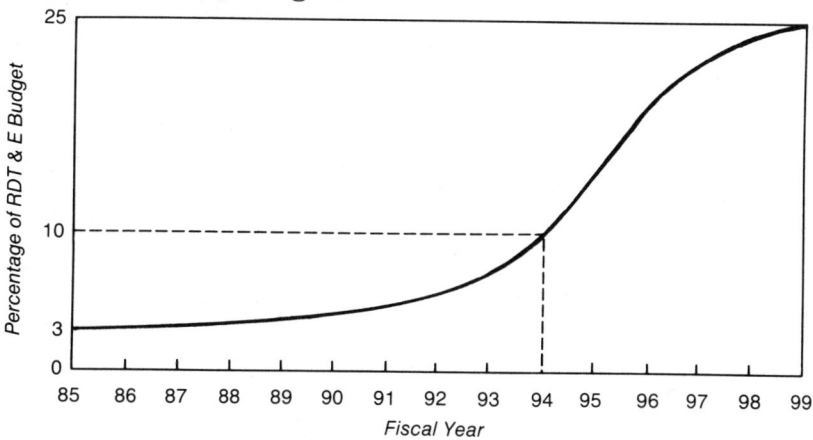

Source: Frank Carlucci, *Annual Report to the Congress, Fiscal Year 1989* (Washington, D.C.: GPO, February 1988).

tematic identification of new collaborative opportunities in advanced research and development, especially where the impact on critical NATO requirements such as FOFA is maximized, has yet to be done. Further, the lack of a coherent policy on technology transfer and technology security clearly hampers planning for new NATO cooperative programs. A large measure of responsibility for the absence of such a framework must rest with the United States, whose inability to coordinate its internal policy on technology security has made a meaningful dialogue with European allies extremely difficult.

BTI and Competitive Strategies are there to be used. If they are to have maximum effect, they cannot be just U.S.-only programs. What does it matter if the United States has married advanced technologies with innovative concepts if its allies have not? The coalition defense has not necessarily been strengthened, because a smart adversary will not attack the defense at its strongest, but at its weakest, points.

The United States has indicated that it is willing to share. The European allies have shown interest. It is now time for action.

New Technology and Arms Control

On April 18, 1986, General Secretary Gorbachev surprised the West by reversing a decades-long position of the Soviet Union and indicating his willingness to engage in arms control negotiations over conventional force in Europe "from the Atlantic to the Urals." NATO quickly welcomed this proposal to energize conventional arms control after more than a decade of frustration at the Mutual and Balanced Force Reduction talks. Since mid-1987, negotiators from NATO and Warsaw Pact countries have been meeting in Vienna to hammer out a mandate for these new "Conventional Stability Talks" (CST).

New and prospective conventional technology is only

one factor that will make NATO-Warsaw Pact arms control talks an extremely complicated business. How NATO handles the issue of new technology will be critical not only for the direction and ultimate success of the negotiations but also for the future of NATO's conventional defense capabilities.

NATO and Warsaw Pact nations have agreed that the major focus of the talks must be the asymmetries inherent in the current force balance. What each side means by asymmetries, however, is a subject on which there is less agreement.

From NATO's perspective, the primary goal of the CST negotiations was defined by NATO foreign ministers in their December 1986 Brussels statement as a "stable" and "secure" level of conventional forces. This goal could be achieved through "the elimination of the capability for surprise attack or for the initiation of large scale offensive action." At their March 1988 summit, NATO heads of government refined that definition by indicating that NATO wanted to concentrate on reductions of the large numbers of Soviet tanks and artillery deployed forward in eastern Europe, weapons in which the Warsaw Pact has an approximate advantage over NATO of three to one.

Although NATO knows in principle what it wants to achieve, it has had trouble agreeing on the price it could or should pay to accomplish it. By the summer of 1988, for example, there was no agreement on whether NATO should accept any significant reductions in its own forces, and, if so, where those reductions should be taken. If reductions on the NATO side are not seen in the alliance's interest, there is also little agreement on what leverage NATO can exert to secure the kinds of reductions from the Warsaw Pact that it thinks necessary to achieve stability.[6]

Meanwhile, the Warsaw Pact believes that NATO also has some asymmetrical advantages that must be rectified. The Pact has expressed concern, for example, over NATO's advantage in advanced combat aircraft. There has also been considerable speculation that the Kremlin is extremely interested in blunting NATO's edge in advanced technology development—if not by stopping the process completely, then by slowing it down considerably. Given the perception that the Soviets have no desire to engage in a high-technology competition with the West that they believe they could not win, the conclusion has been suggested that the Kremlin might entertain a deal in which reductions of its tanks and artillery in eastern Europe are exchanged for limitations on the development of Western technology. Precisely which fields they would target are unclear, but speculation has centered on standoff weapons technology and submarine-launched cruise missiles, the technologies that would allow NATO to extend its attack deeper into Warsaw Pact territory.

NATO has initially indicated that it has little desire to agree to any sort of technology limitation. The West's traditional reliance on its technological capability to offset its numerical inferiority is reinforced by skepticism about anyone's ability to define adequately verifiable limits to technology development.

NATO's approach to the technology issue in the forthcoming talks is crucial. How NATO deals with technology will be felt throughout the force structure and will have considerable implications for other arms control negotiations as well. Equally important, it will also be a major factor in shaping the future relationship between the nuclear and conventional components of NATO's deterrent. There is a complex process of interaction in which arms control and force-improvement decisions affect one another, not only horizontally on the level of the deterrent (whether nuclear or conventional) but also vertically between the nuclear and conventional levels. There has already been some concern, for example, that the Intermediate-Range Nuclear Force (INF) Treaty could have unforeseen consequences for NATO's conventional capabilities. One consequence that was discussed was the treaty's impact on NATO's ability to deploy such systems as the ground-launched Tacit Rainbow antiradar UAV with a range that is prohibited by the treaty.

Great care must be taken to ensure that attractive technological options are not lost because arms control decisions were not embedded in the broader security context that relates arms control positions to force modernization and budget decisions.

This relationship between technology and conventional arms control remains largely unexplored. There has not yet been a definition of what contributions can be made to European security by focusing on technological limitations in arms control negotiations. It remains one area in which further study is urgently needed.

According to historian Martin van Creveld,

> World War II witnessed the coming of age of that intimate alliance between science, government, and the military that has been such a conspicuous feature of the post-1945 period. War, which 25 years earlier had been extended from the battlefields into the factories, now reached even further into the laboratories, and it was here that it was often decided.[7]

There is no doubt that the laboratory has become a critical battleground of future wars. The twofold challenge to NATO policymakers is the integration of new technology into tactical and operational concepts and the adaptation of those same concepts to new technological opportunities. The most dangerous attitude, therefore, is not one that is antitechnology but antichange — an unquestioning acceptance of existing concepts as the best ones possible, even with new technology.

The bureaucratic inertia of large institutions prompts resistance to change. In this respect, NATO has been no different from many other large international organizations. At the same time, NATO has sometimes demonstrated a remarkable flexibility in finding ways around bureaucratic barriers when the issues are critical.

Moreover, there is reason for optimism. NATO has taken several important steps in recent years, such as development of the Conceptual Military Framework, introduction of the FOFA concept, passage of the Nunn-Roth-Warner cooperative research and development amendment, and adoption of the Conventional Armaments Planning System. Solid building blocks as a possible foundation for the future exist in the BTI and the Competitive Strategies Study.

If NATO is to make full use of the contribution that technology can offer to continued deterrence and defense, NATO policymakers will need all the ingenuity they can muster in making the critical decisions about which technologies should be pursued and how they should be applied. In a complex technological environment replete with challenge, the leaders of NATO's member nations can do no less than demonstrate the same human creativity in its council chambers that their scientists and engineers have demonstrated in their laboratories to spark the technological explosion the world now watches.

Notes

Chapter 1

1. General Robert T. March, USAF, "A Preview of the Technology Revolution," *Air Force* 67, no. 8 (August 1984): 43.

2. "Silicon Valley, Move Over," *Armed Forces Journal International* 123, no. 2 (June 1986): 46.

3. "The Pentagon Will Settle for Not-So-Super VHSIC Chip," *Electronics*, April 28, 1988, p. 34.

4. Cited in "Electronic Technology to Dominate Next Generation of Weapons Systems," *Aviation Week and Space Technology*, June 6, 1988, p. 81.

5. "The Technology of the Time: Smaller is Faster and Smarter," *Atlanta Constitution*, May 17, 1988, p. 1.

6. Ibid.

7. "Silicon Valley, Move Over," 41–54.

8. "Electronic Technology to Dominate," 81.

9. David Hobbs, *NATO and New Technology*, Washington, D.C.: American University Press in cooperation with the Atlantic Council of the United States, forthcoming 1988.

10. "Crucial Role for Electronics," Survey of European High Technology, *Financial Times*, April 13, 1988, p. iv.

11. "Defense Contractors Target Electronics," *High Technology* (July 1988), 30.

12. Tom Forester, "The Materials Revolution," *Futurist* (July–August 1988), 22–25.

13. Ibid.

14. Richard Corrigan, "The Fiber Optics Future," *National Journal* 18, no. 23 (June 7, 1986), 1371.

15. For a discussion of the potential military application of Artificial Intelligence, see the special section of *Aviation Week and Space Technology*, April 22, 1985, pp. 41–84.

16. For a good discussion of the cumulative impact of changes in these areas, see John Yochelson, ed., *Keeping Pace: U.S. Policies and Global Economic Change* (Cambridge, Mass.: Ballinger Publishing Company, 1988).

17. François Heisbourg, "Europe at the Turn of the Millennium: Decline or Rebirth?" *Washington Quarterly* 10, no. 1 (Winter 1987), 45.

18. François Heisbourg, "Private Sector Arrangements: A Pattern for the Future?" a paper prepared for the Conference on High Technology Western Security and Economic Growth: An Agenda for the Future, sponsored by the U.S. Missions to NATO, the European Communities, the Organization for Economic Cooperation and Development, and the U.S. Embassy in Brussels, Belgium, February 6–8, 1986, p. 6.

19. Daniel Roos of the Massachusetts Institute of Technology cited in "The Titans of High Technology – Japan and The United States – A Survey," *Economist*, August 23, 1986, p. S16.

20. "NAS President Frank Press Calls on Science to Set Its Own Priorities," *Chemical and Engineering News*, June 13, 1988, p. 28.

21. "U.S. Pursues Competitive Edge with Joint Research," *Baltimore Sun*, July 25, 1986, p. C-1.

22. Roos, "The Titans of High Technology," S14.

23. Harold B. Malmgren, "Innovation and the Global Economic Environment," in Yochelson, *Keeping Pace*.

24. Ibid.

25. For a more detailed assessment of the current situation, see Robert Banks, rapporteur, "Draft Interim Report," Subcommittee on Advanced Technology and Technology Transfer, North Atlantic Assembly, STC/AT (88)1, Brussels, May 1988, pp. 31–77.

26. Ibid., 66.

27. Roos, "The Titans of High Technology," S6–S7.

28. Ibid., S7.

29. The observations of both men were reported in "U.S., Ja-

pan Approach New Era in Service and Technology Relations,"
Chemical and Engineering News, April 11, 1988, p. 14.

30. Heisbourg, "Europe at the Turn of the Millennium," 45.

31. Ibid., 15.

32. Ibid.

33. Michael Moodie and Robert Windsor, "Managing Technological Change: An Alliance Imperative," Alliance Paper no. 12
(Washington, D.C.: Atlantic Council of the United States in cooperation with the U.S. Mission to NATO, 1986), 3.

34. Cited in North Atlantic Assembly (NAA) "Draft Interim
Report," 32.

35. Ibid.

36. The Framework Program and the other EC cooperative
R&D efforts are described in Ibid., 34–52.

37. "Esprit lifts European info-tech," *Sunday Times* (London), June 12, 1988, p. D-13.

38. NAA "Draft Interim Report," 36.

39. Ibid., 47–48.

40. "Brussels Studies Funding Plans to Develop Chips," *Financial Times*, July 12, 1988, p. A-1.

41. "Collaboration: A Change in Attitudes," Europe's High
Technology Survey, *Financial Times*, April 13, 1988, p. II.

42. Cited in "Tonic that failed to give a lift," *Financial Times*,
September 29, 1986, p. 23.

43. NAA "Draft Interim Report," 72.

44. "When the Pentagon Turns Consumer," *Financial Times*,
August 14, 1986, p. 11.

Chapter 2

1. This chapter is based on the author's "New Theater Conventional Technologies," a paper prepared for the Core Seminar
Series on Technology, Strategy and the Arms Control Process of
the Woodrow Wilson Center for International Scholars, The
Smithsonian Institution, May 1988.

2. Michael Handel, "Clausewitz and the Age of Technology,"
Journal of Strategic Studies 9 (June/September 1986): 60–61.

3. Ibid.

4. Admiral John Jervis, made Lord St. Vincent for his stun-
ning victory at Cape St. Vincent, condemned Prime Minister Pitt

as "the greatest fool alive" for trying to push the torpedo on the Royal Navy. Lord Kitchener dismissed the tank as a "toy," and as late as 1915, Sir Douglas Haig disparaged the impact of the machine gun. For more on this point, see the chapter on "Technology Strategy," in David Abshire, *Preventing World War III: A Realistic Grand Strategy* (New York: Harper and Row, forthcoming).

5. Handel, "Clausewitz and the Age of Technology," 73.

6. Alan Gropman, "Continuities: The United States Air Force of 2005," a paper prepared for the Conference on Resources, Technology, and Future Battlefields, sponsored by the Center for Strategic and International Studies (CSIS), Washington, D.C., October 27–29, 1987 (hereafter referred to as the CSIS Future Battlefields Conference), 9.

7. Benjamin J. Lambeth, "Pitfalls in Force Planning: Structuring America's Tactical Air Arm," *International Security* 10, no. 2 (Fall 1985): 90.

8. François Heisbourg, "Conventional Defense: Europe's Constraints and Opportunities," *The Conventional Defense of Europe: New Technologies and New Strategies*, Andrew Pierre, ed. (New York: Council on Foreign Relations, 1986): 83.

9. *Defense News*, May 2, 1988, p. 17.

10. Norman Friedman, "The Naval Battlefield of the Future," a paper prepared for the CSIS Future Battlefields Conference, 8.

11. Ibid.

12. Ibid., 10.

13. For further elaboration of this point, see Abshire, "Technology Strategy."

14. For such a comprehensive discussion, see Hobbs, *NATO and New Technology*.

15. Daniel J. Kaufman, "Evolution of the Land Battlefield," a paper prepared for CSIS Future Battlefields Conference, 9.

16. "New Light Fighter Could Augment Stealth Fleet," *Air Force Times*, May 30, 1988, p. 35.

17. John Macrostie, "Resources, Technology and Future Battlefields," a paper prepared for the CSIS Future Battlefields Conference, 5.

18. Admiral William Small, "The Evolution of Maritime Battlefields," a paper prepared for CSIS Future Battlefields Conference.

19. Macrostie, "Resources, Technology and Future Battlefields," 7.

20. "FOG-M: The Fiber Optic Guided Missile," *Defense Science* (May 1988), 45.

21. Kaufman, "Evolution of the Land Battlefield."

22. Ibid.

23. Hobbs, *NATO and New Technology*.

24. Ibid.

25. Ibid.

26. Ibid.

27. Macrostie, "Resources, Technology and Future Battlefields," 5.

28. Martin van Creveld, *Command in War* (Cambridge, Mass.: Harvard University Press, 1985), 267.

29. Kaufman, "Evolution of the Land Battlefield," 15.

30. Heisbourg, "Conventional Defense," 83.

31. Admiral Harry Train, "The Sea Battlefield," a paper prepared for the CSIS Future Battlefields Conference.

32. Kaufman, "Evolution of the Land Battlefield," 24.

33. Fred H. Wisely, "Battlefield Space," a paper prepared for the CSIS Future Battlefields Conference.

34. "Leclerc Impresses French Officials," *Defense News*, April 18, 1988, p. 10.

35. Colonel Richard W. Whaton, "Survivable Hardware Coming? You Can Bet On It!" *Field Artillery Journal* (April 1988), 12.

36. Kaufman, "Evolution of the Land Battlefield," 23.

37. "New Light Fighter," 35.

38. John Paul Newport, Jr., "A Growing Gap in Software," *Fortune*, April 28, 1986, p. 133.

39. Julian S. Lake, "ATF: Out of the Shadows," *Defense Science* (May 1988), 37.

40. "Stealth Technology," *Los Angeles Times*, May 16, 1988, p. II-4.

41. "Cost of Stealth Bombers Soars to $450 Million Each," *Washington Post*, May 15, 1988, p. 1.

42. "EFA Stealth Technology May Take Years to Develop," *Defense News*, April 25, 1988, p. 8.

43. "Cost of Stealth Bombers Soars."

44. "Stealth Technology," II-4.

45. Quoted in *Defense News*, April 18, 1988, p. 10.

46. For a review of some of the major developments in military satellites, see James W. Rawles, "Military Satellites: The Next Generation," *Defense Electronics*, May 1988, p. 46ff.

47. Hobbs, *NATO and New Technology*.

48. Nicholas L. Johnson, "Space Control and Soviet Military Strategy," *Defense Electronics*, May 1988, p. 75.

49. Ibid. See also Colin S. Gray, "ASAT for Space Control," *Defense Science* (June 1988), 38.

50. Johnson, "Space Control," 75.

51. Wisely, "Battlefield Space."

52. Ibid.

53. D. J. Alberts, "New Technology and Tactical Aircraft: A Tactics Revolution Ahead?" *Military Technology*, June 1986, p. 93.

54. Ibid.

55. For the best analysis of the evolution of logistical systems, see Martin van Creveld, *Supplying War* (Cambridge: Cambridge University Press, 1977).

56. Heisbourg, "Conventional Defense," 84.

Chapter 3

1. *Soviet Military Power: An Assessment of the Threat 1988* (Washington, D.C.: Department of Defense, April 1988), 143.

2. "Second Sale of Toshiba Technology to Soviets Surfaces," *Detroit News*, March 13, 1988, p. 22A.

3. *Soviet Military Power 1988*, 140.

4. *Soviet Acquisition of Militarily Significant Western Technology: An Update*, (Washington, D.C., U.S. Government, September 1985), 6.

5. In 1980, roughly 400 million rubles ($640 million) were saved, according to Central Intelligence Agency (CIA) estimates, and a total savings of at least 1.4 billion rubles was achieved in the five years between 1976 and 1980. Ibid., 10.

6. Ibid., 8.

7. Ibid.

8. The CIA study lists literally hundreds of Soviet weapons systems benefiting from Western technology and products. It argues that an average of more than 5,000 Soviet military projects per year in the early 1980s benefited from Western hardware and technical documents. See *Soviet Acquisition*, 31–34.

9. *Soviet Military Power 1988*, pp. 140, 149.

10. Some examples of their sources are the enormous number

of unclassified documents and technical journals, the unclassified documents of the Commerce Department's National Technical Information Service (a data base that includes information on the design, evaluation, and testing of U.S. weapon systems), participation in scientific conferences, and other academic activities such as exchanges.

11. See *Soviet Acquisition of Western Technology* (Washington, D.C., U.S. Government, April 1982), 3.

12. *Soviet Military Power 1988*, 143.

13. Henry Nau, "International Technology Transfer," *Washington Quarterly* 8, no. 1 (Winter 1985): 58–60.

14. Ibid., 59.

15. See the edited transcript of the presentation by Dr. Angela Stent on "Differences Within NATO over East-West Trade and the Impact on Eastern Europe," to the Johns Hopkins Foreign Policy Institute U.S.-Soviet Trade Roundtable, Johns Hopkins School of Advanced International Studies, February 18, 1988.

16. "Europeans Protest US Export Controls," *Science*, May 11, 1984, p. 579.

17. Cited by Malcolm Gladwell, "A National Interest in Global Markets," *Insight*, June 29, 1987, p. 10.

18. Richard Rode, "High Tech: A Janus Face," *Bulletin of Peace Proposals*, no. 2 (1986): 186.

19. "How far should US go to regulate its technology exports?" *Christian Science Monitor*, May 16, 1984, p. 16.

20. Ibid.

21. Gladwell, "A National Interest," 10.

22. Ibid., 11.

23. Ibid.

24. Quoted in "NATO Friction is Sharpening Over Technology Export Issue," *International Herald Tribune*, October 27, 1987, p. 6.

25. "Washington Counters Soviet pilfering of its high-tech know-how," *Christian Science Monitor*, May 18, 1984, p. 14.

26. Cited in "Preventing Technology Theft," *Defense Science and Electronics*, January 1987, p. 69.

27. Ibid.

28. "Washington Counters Soviet pilfering," 14.

29. "National Science Academy Study Heats Up Dispute Between High Tech Exporters, Defense Department," *Los Angeles Times*, January 19, 1987, p. IV-1.

30. See Richard Gross, "Technology Transfer: A Losing Battle?" *Defense Science*, March 1988, p. 9. In another case, the DOD accused the Commerce Department of deliberately misleading the president to secure approval of the export of digitally controlled wire bonders that would wire in microcircuits. See "Commerce Department Nears Decision on Technical Trade Misinformation Charges," *Defense News*, March 20, 1988, p. 23.

31. "New Dispute Seen Looming over DOD Effort to take Export Review From State," *Inside the Pentagon*, July 3, 1987, p. 6.

32. "Pentagon Duels Over Jet Engines," *Washington Times*, June 21, 1988, p. 3.

33. Cited in Michael Moodie and Robert Windsor, "Managing Technological Change: An Alliance Imperative," 12.

34. Cited by *New York Times*, February 15, 1988, p. 7.

35. *Wall Street Journal*, January 29, 1988, p. 16.

36. Gross, "Technology Transfer: A Losing Battle?" 8.

37. "Come On, COCOM," *Economist*, July 11, 1987, p. 17.

38. "Four Executives in France are Arrested for Exports of Technology to the Soviets," *Wall Street Journal*, April 25, 1988, p. 23.

39. *Washington Times*, June 6, 1988, p. 1.

Chapter 4

1. Presentation by Lord Carrington to a meeting cosponsored by the Eurogroup and CSIS, May 1987.

2. For a more detailed discussion of structural disarmament, see Thomas A. Callaghan, Jr., "The Structural Disarmament of NATO," *NATO Review*, no. 3 (June 1984): 1–6.

3. Frank C. Carlucci, Department of Defense, "Report on Allied Contributions to the Common Defense," A Report to the U.S. Congress, April 1988, p. 9.

4. Cited in Frank T. J. Bray and Michael Moodie, *Defense Technology in the Atlantic Alliance: Competition or Collaboration?* (Cambridge, Mass.: Institute for Foreign Policy Analysis, April 1977), 5.

5. Thomas A. Callaghan, Jr., *US/European Economic Cooperation in Civil and Military Technology: An Issues Oriented Report* (Arlington, Va.: Ex-Im Tech, Inc., 1974).

6. See David M. Abshire, "Arms Cooperation in NATO," *Armed Forces Journal International* 123, no. 6 (December 1985): 66.

7. See "Industry-to-Industry International Armaments Cooperation, Phase 1, NATO Europe," A Report of the Science Board Task Force of the Department of Defense, June 1983.

8. Abshire, "Arms Cooperation in NATO," 68.

9. Quoted in Michael Moodie and Robert Windsor, Managing Technological Change: An Alliance Imperative," 23.

10. Frank C. Carlucci, "Support of NATO Strategy in the 1990's," A Report to the U.S. Congress in compliance with Public Law 100-80, Department of Defense, January, 1988, p. xv.

11. News Release, Office of Assistant Secretary of Defense (Public Affairs), "DOD Announces Formation of Defense Cooperation Working Group," No. 34–87, January 21, 1987.

12. David M. Abshire, *NATO on the Move*, Alliance Paper no. 6 (Washington, D.C.: Atlantic Council of the United States in cooperation with the U.S. Mission to NATO, 1985), 21.

13. "FRG Pullout World Doom MSOW Effort, Officials Say," *Defense News*, July 18, 1988, p. 4.

14. The Right Honourable The Lord Carrington, "NATO Armaments Planning," A Memo to the Permanent Representatives (Council) of NATO, May 13, 1987, p. 2.

15. "Statement on the Defence Estimates 1988, Part 1," presented to Parliament by the Secretary of State for Defence by Command of Her Majesty, London, 1988, p. 39.

16. John F. Morton and Ben Schemmer, "Congress Backs Big Boosts in U.S. Two-Way Street Buys," *Armed Forces Journal* 125, no. 5 (December 1987): 72.

17. "TI-Rafale Deal Reflects Technology Transfer Analyses," *Aerospace Daily*, January 22, 1988, p. 109.

18. "Electronic Technology to Dominate Next Generation of Weapons Systems," *Aviation Week & Space Technology*, June 6, 1988, pp. 82–83.

19. "Towards a Stronger Europe," a Report of the Independent Study Team of the Independent European Programme Group (IEPG) (Brussels: IEPG, December 1986), 1.

20. "Comrades in Arms Discover an Unsung Detente," *Financial Times*, July 1, 1988, p. 6.

21. Ibid.

22. IEPG, "Towards a Stronger Europe," 8–12.

23. "Europe's Plan to Build New Fighter Plane Puts Western Firms on Cutthroat Course," *Wall Street Journal*, May 23, 1988, p. 16.

24. "West Europeans Agree to Build Fighters," *Washington Post*, May 17, 1988, p. 19.

25. "West Germany to Scratch Programs for EFA," *Defense News*, May 30, 1988, p. 1.

26. "EEC Mulls Tax on U.S. Hardware," *Defense News*, May 23, 1988, p. 1.

27. "Keeping Europe on the IT Map," *Financial Times*, May 18, 1988.

28. "West Europeans are inching towards a common market in arms," *Financial Times*, April 15, 1988, p. 15.

29. This would make Daimler-MBB approximately twice the size of United Technologies, ranked as the largest U.S. aerospace concern. "West Germany's New Military Giant," *Financial Times*, July 13, 1988, p. 14.

30. Philip Revgin, "US, European Firms Prepare for 1992 Deadline," *Europe* (April 1988), 18.

31. See remarks by Robert L. Kirk, chairman and CEO of Allied-Signal Aerospace Company, to the Annual Meeting of the American Institute of Aeronautics and Astronautics, Arlington, Virginia, May 4, 1988.

32. IEPG, "Towards A Stronger Europe," 14.

Conclusion

1. Senate Armed Services Committee, *National Defense Authorization Act for Fiscal Year 1988 and 1989*, 100th Congress, 1st session (Washington, D.C.: GPO, 1987), 124.

2. See DOD Statement on the Balanced Technology Initiative by Dr. Robert C. Duncan, director, Defense Research and Engineering, to the Senate Armed Services Committee, April 11, 1988, pp. 3-4.

3. "NATO: Meeting the Coming Challenge – an Alliance Action Plan for Conventional Improvements and Armaments Cooperation," prepared by the Project on a Resources Strategy for the United States and Its Allies, CSIS, December 18, 1987, p. 37.

4. Frank C. Carlucci, Department of Defense, "Report on Allied Contributions to the Common Defense," 10.

5. "Avionics Firms Increase Investments, But Market Growth Expected to Slow," *Aviation Week & Space Technology*, May 30, 1988, p. 72.

6. Some commentators argue, for example, that those reductions must be at least on a 5 : 1 basis. See James A. Thomson and Nanette C. Gantz, "Conventional Arms Control Revisited: Objectives in the New Phase," *Conventional Arms Control and the Security of Europe*, Uwe Nerlich and James A. Thomson, eds. (Boulder and London: Westview Press, 1988), 108–123.

7. Martin van Creveld, "Turning Points in Twentieth Century War," *Washington Quarterly* 4, no. 3 (Summer 1981): 6.

Index